PROVOCATIVE
GRACE

PROVOCATIVE GRACE

The Challenge
in Jesus' Words

ROBERT CORIN MORRIS

UPPER
ROOM BOOKS®
NASHVILLE

PROVOCATIVE GRACE
The Challenge in Jesus' Words
Copyright © 2006 by Robert Corin Morris
All rights reserved.

Unless otherwise marked, scripture quotations are from the New Revised Standard Version Bible, copyright 1989, Division of Christian Education of the National Council of the Churches of Christ in the United States of America. Used by permission. All rights reserved.

Scripture quotations marked NKJV are taken from the New King James Version®. Copyright © 1982 by Thomas Nelson, Inc. Used by permission. All rights reserved.

Scripture quotations marked REB are taken from the *Revised English Bible,* copyright © Oxford University Press and Cambridge University Press 1989. All rights reserved.

Scripture quotations marked NLT are taken from the *Holy Bible, New Living Translation,* copyright © 1996. Used by permission of Tyndale House Publishers, Inc. Wheaton, Illinois 60189. All rights reserved

Scripture noted THE MESSAGE from *The Message* by Eugene H. Peterson, copyright © 1993, 1994, 1995, 1996, 200, 2001, 2002. Used by permission of NavPress Publishing Group. All rights reserved.

King James Version is designated KJV. AT indicates Author Translation; AP indicates Author Paraphrase.

At the time of publication all Web sites referenced in this book were valid. However, due to the fluid nature of the Internet some addresses may have changed or the content may no longer be relevant.

Cover and interior design: Gore Studio, Inc., Nashville
Cover image: © Photodisc
First printing: 2006

LIBRARY OF CONGRESS CATALOGING-IN-PUBLICATION DATA
Morris, Robert Corin
    Provocative grace : the challenge in Jesus' words / Robert Corin Morris.
        p. cm.
    ISBN 0-8358-9848-2   ISBN 978-0-8358-9848-5
    1. Christian life—Biblical teaching. 2. Jesus Christ—Teachings. I. Title.
    BS2417.C5M67 2006
    232.9'54—dc22   2006008615

Printed in the United States of America

To Barnaby, Daniel, and Alec,

fellow apprentices on the Way.

May your journeys be long and rich!

CONTENTS

ACKNOWLEDGMENTS

Writing a book, I am discovering, is the work of a lifetime. As the subject is tackled, seeds planted decades back, and long since sprouted as plants, bear fresh fruit for the project. So the contributors to the book are numberless and beyond naming: sermons heard, books read, classes taught, and comments from participants so adopted as my own that the original sources have been forgotten. But a few who are remembered deserve grateful mention.

My fundamentalist grandfather, Jesse Andrew Mullins, taught me to love the Bible, and the progressive minister of my teen years, Norman H. Beaman, helped loosen the hold of fundamentalist ideology on the now-beloved text. Anglican biblical scholars like William Temple taught me to read scripture in the context of a world-embracing theology and the whole sweep of Christian tradition, and radicals like Rudolf Bultmann, whose historical skepticism I rejected, nonetheless made me think hard about the essence of Jesus' message.

Teaching Bible has been a central passion for over forty years, and numerous people whisper in the back of my mind. Most recently, my Friday and Saturday morning "Bible for a New Day" classes have been filled with engaged, inquiring folk eager to explore the implications of Jesus' teaching for themselves. Special thanks goes to my group of readers, whose feedback has been most helpful: Barbara Adams, David Bate Jr., Bob and Bobbie Festa, Kathleen Locke, Lori McConnell, Ellie Muska, Daniel Nelson, Barnaby Reidel, Jane Riedel, Jane Sullivan, Juli Towell, and Sue Zivi.

Most of all, my wife of thirty-six years, Suzanne, deserves my unqualified gratitude for acting as sounding board, proofreader, loving critic, and book writer's widow for too many long days and nights.

Looking for a Fresh Vision of Jesus

A Few Words about This Approach

A RESTLESS SEARCH for a fresh vision of Jesus has once more emerged, as it does in times of great change. You may sense it too. Millions seem to want to see the prophet of Nazareth from an angle different than their Sunday school training or the doctrinally based conventions of piety. This search, bolstered by best sellers and scholarly tomes that claim the New Testament has plastered over the real Jesus with an ecclesiastical substitute, peers beneath, behind, or beyond the surface of the New Testament texts to find a Jesus "hidden" by the second generation of Christians who wrote them or examines alternative Gospels suppressed by the church.[1]

I believe we do need a fresh vision of Jesus. But I am convinced, for reasons given below and in the afterword, that the "hidden Jesus" lurks—in plain sight—right in front of our eyes in the pages of the four traditional Gospels.

More than new texts or a Jesus hidden behind the surface of the New Testament, we need a new angle of vision on Gospel sayings obscured by nothing more than familiarity with them. Only then will we recognize the Gospels' startling challenges to the human heart and mind. I've spent over three decades of active teaching ministry dedicated to seeing the Gospel texts with fresh eyes, what Zen Buddhists call "beginner's mind." Using a variety of lenses—comparative religion, depth psychology, new historical information, and imaginative meditating on Gospel scenes—can sometimes startle us into new amazement at the wisdom of sayings grown stale by repetition or imprisoned on a particular dogmatic framework.

I have included a few sayings from one of those alternative Gospels, Thomas, for reasons explained in the afterword, but this book, for the most part, is about the Jesus portrayed in the four New Testament Gospels—Matthew, Mark, Luke, and John—and the impact of some of his sayings in the lives of ordinary people like you and me. I have come to believe that these words can challenge any human being to grow toward greater maturity as a member of the human family and a participant in God's loving and just reign on earth.

AN INVITATION TO ALL SEEKERS

Whether you are a devout Christian, an inquiring seeker, or a rank skeptic, if you wish to explore the teaching of Jesus, this book is intended for you. The book is also written for any who walk one of the other great spiritual pathways, whether Jewish, Hindu, Buddhist, Confucian, or modern ethical humanist. Jesus the rabbi, teacher, prophet, and founder of a world religion is too important a teacher of human wisdom to limit the impact of his words to a tight circle of Christian believers, however numerous. Much of the moral core of Jesus' sayings appears in other traditions as well. Followers of many paths can find in this core a common ground of human values that transcends doctrinal differences. Discussion of that moral basis of human life needs to include Jesus' words.

What you believe about Jesus certainly has significance, but you don't have to accept the Christian creeds to begin listening to Jesus or putting some of his teachings into practice. He deserves, at the least, the same respect accorded any person wise in the ways of living. Jesus himself states that acting on his words is far more important than merely saying "Lord" to him (see Matt. 7:21).

Therefore, this book focuses on the words of the man Jesus, not on theological beliefs about his divinity, the exact nature of which has been long debated in the Christian family.[2] As a believer, it's second nature for me to hear in the human words of Jesus nothing less than the Divine Wisdom itself. They demand that I listen deeply, especially to the teachings that startle, perplex, or offend me most. But whatever you believe about Jesus' ultimate identity, I hope this book will help you give his challenges for human life a serious hearing.

I will deal with what Jesus means by "believing in" him and his claims in a later chapter, but for the most part I'm simply concerned that we let the man provoke us into looking at how we're living our lives, personally and socially. I would consider a Buddhist or a Hindu, a Jew or a Jain, a seeker or an agnostic who sincerely follows some of Jesus' teachings to be part of a wide fellowship of disciples or apprentices to Jesus' Way that stretches beyond the borders of formal Christianity.

As you will quickly discover, an attitude of respectful listening need not involve uncritical acceptance or blind faith. Honestly reacting against something Jesus says is better than submitting uncritically. The disciples debated with Jesus. Their debate follows the pattern found in a whole strand of biblical story and rabbinical storytelling in which God as a patient teacher quite willingly engages the human spirit in dialogue.[3] This book invites you to just such an engagement by showing how key sayings and stories have challenged and changed me and other people who have graciously shared their experiences.

ENCOUNTERING THE "REAL" JESUS

The text of the four Gospels is treated without any reference to scholarly debates about how much any passage reflects the "Jesus of history" and how much reflects the "Christ of faith"—that is, the later reflection of the church.[4] I do not reject the overwhelming consensus of scholars that a developmental process formed the Gospel tradition and culminated in our written Gospels, but I remain more than a bit skeptical of modern attempts to rate particular Gospel sayings or stories as more or less authentic.

Scholarly trends come and go. In cycles reaching back over two centuries, each period of historical skepticism has been followed by renewed respect for the historical roots of the Gospels.[5] If you're interested in my opinions about that controversy, you may wish to read the comments in the afterword.

Meanwhile, the texts of the four Gospels remain, and in them the man lovingly encountered by millions through these texts over the centuries. Furthermore, this is the figure with whom non-Christians have had to reckon. My bias favors this "common Jesus" rather than a picture of Jesus edited according to the particular scholarly theory of any age or author. I believe you can discover more about Jesus by reading and rereading the texts, whole and entire as they stand, than in any editing of them. Smoothing out the rough edges and seeming contradictions of the Gospel narrative to produce a more consistent portrait runs the danger of making Jesus less complex than any really human being.

Occasionally I've inserted quotations from the New Testament's apostolic letters because they are our earliest commentaries on Jesus' teaching. For the same reason, a few sayings from the noncanonical Gospel of Thomas are included because they amplify for me the meaning of familiar sayings.

Rather than delve deep into these alternative Gospels, however, I've chosen to stay close to the Jesus Christians throughout the ages have had in common. As far as I am concerned, the real Jesus, the one who can make an impact on our lives, leaps into life in these interpretative encounters. Such encounters are part of the mystery of the Resurrection, one of the ways the man Christians honor as Christ—God's decisive messenger to humanity—continues to affect history.

The Christian tradition stays alive through the encounter of each disciple, each community, and each era with the memory of Jesus contained in the sayings and stories. Inevitably, then, this book presents my own angle on Jesus, so personal, in fact, I've even presumed to paraphrase Jesus' words in addition to a standard translation of each saying. Paraphrasing, not just parroting, promotes internalizing someone else's ideas. I encourage you to check out multiple translations, as I have, and try paraphrasing the Gospel words as a way of pondering what Jesus says.

There are potentially as many versions of Jesus in existence as there are people who encounter the story. We face not only the danger of subjectivity but also the possibility of creative responses to Jesus arising for a wide variety of new situations. I believe we're meant to learn from past interpretations, share and discuss our new insights with one another, and debate how best to follow Jesus in our own time and place. The church itself is meant to be the place where that discussion flourishes, not a haven for those who just say, "Yes, Boss" to the Master Teacher.

Saving truth can be discovered only in actual living, not out of a book or even from a teacher's mouth. Wrestling with Jesus' challenges has played a major role in my coming to what maturity as a human being I may have. Jesus has been my lifelong provocateur, prompting me to explore how his sayings actually work out in daily life. I've loved him, resented him, argued with him, and, in the end, found more wisdom in his sayings than any first impression could have revealed.

Whoever you are and whatever you believe about Jesus, my hope for you is this—that you can encounter his words afresh and through them, God's loving grace, which is more than a bit provocative.

CHAPTER 1

Jesus the Provocateur

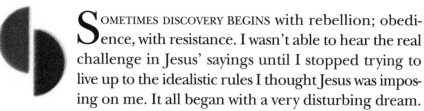

SOMETIMES DISCOVERY BEGINS with rebellion; obedience, with resistance. I wasn't able to hear the real challenge in Jesus' sayings until I stopped trying to live up to the idealistic rules I thought Jesus was imposing on me. It all began with a very disturbing dream.

In the dream I was a boy, say six or seven years old, craning my neck to look up the side of a gigantic, steel-clad skyscraper so tall I couldn't even see the top of it. In the presence of this looming structure, which I was somehow supposed to climb, I felt small and inadequate. Intimidated, I lowered my gaze to the six-story base of the building, upon which was emblazoned the inscription: "Thou shalt love the Lord thy God with all thy heart and soul and mind and strength and thy neighbor as thyself."

All? my dream self thought, heart sinking. *Does it really mean all? How can I ever corral all those conflicting desires and impulses in me into one, pure, simple "all"?* I awoke anxious and agitated, and a blunt prayer arose: *It's just too high; I can't attain it. I need to start with something I can actually do.*

This was all before I came to realize that Jesus was neither a rule maker nor an idealist but a provocateur. His sayings are not rules to live up to but challenges to live into. Rather than impossible ideals imposed on us, they are provocations to grow step-by-step, by trial-and-error learning, into the best possibilities of our nature.

I have not come to make you comfortable.

Do not think that I have come to bring peace.
—MATTHEW 10:34

Make no mistake. Jesus is out to provoke us. While this is not the Jesus I learned about in Sunday school, it is the man I began to encounter after my dream and much honest prayer had broken the shackles of pious idealism. The Jesus of the Gospel records, in all his modes of encountering people—as prophet, healer, wisdom teacher, mystic, social critic, and nonviolent revolutionary—is a disturber of our immaturities, one who challenges us to find and use our strengths. A master craftsman in the skills that can make us strong in love, generous in service, and abundant in joy, he wants to spur us into a maturity that can collaborate with the Love that gave us birth. This Love seeks partners in making real "the kingdom" or reign of God which heals the hurts and develops the life of this world.

Either in spite of his provocative words or because of them, Jesus got invited to dinner a lot, unlike his solitary, austere, denunciatory cousin, John the Baptist. But Jesus was not an easy guest to have around. You never knew when the conversation would become disturbing. He might ask you why the guest list didn't include the kind of people who couldn't possibly give you such a good meal in return (Luke 14:1-14). Or some disreputable woman from the village might be blessed for washing his feet at your table in full sight of your distinguished guests and the surrounding village gaggle, gathered to watch the important people eat (Luke 7:36-50).

Yet something about Jesus kept the invitations coming. I believe it was because the spirit of these provocations was so patently loving. I don't believe Jesus delivered scolding judgments in that carping, righteous tone of voice that characterizes up-tight moralists. Rather, he was calling out to another person's heart to wake up and listen to truths that could make for wholeness. He might even inquire of the hostess why she was working herself into a hysteria of miserable fatigue when the meal could have been simpler and still appreciated.

Generations of women have quietly bridled, I know, at Jesus' telling his friend Martha of Bethany that "one dish" would have been enough for dinner rather than the feast she's providing. The Gospel impression of him implies he liked food enough to be grateful for good cooking. When he says, "Martha, Martha, you are worried and distracted by many things," he's trying to wake his friend out of her self-inflicted misery, not criticize her hostess skills or disparage her devotion. (See Luke 10:38-42.)

I've known more than one Martha, male and female, so intent on everything being absolutely perfect and over-the-top that he or she not only isn't able to enjoy the party but actually dampens the good spirits. The Greek words used for "worried and distracted" indicate an extremity of inner agitation and misery, not just a bit of fussing. Martha's abject misery flashes out, from behind her bustle, at her sister for daring to step out of a woman's proper role of service to sit among the disciples. *How dare she!* Martha seems to think, in spite of the fact that the hostess probably has the help of any number of neighbor women honored to be serving the prominent teacher who has come to Martha's house.[1]

I've got a bit of a Martha in me. I know the misery that excessive pursuit of the perfect can cause. Jesus' challenge to Martha aims to deliver her from the prison of the "need to be needed—whether one is needed or not." That doesn't mean she and Jesus didn't have, let's say, a bit of a discussion that goes unrecorded: an earful from the aggrieved Martha; reassurance from Jesus that she is loved, appreciated; tears; and then (at least in my fantasy, which is admittedly anachronistic) Jesus helps with the cleanup. (We know he washed feet. Why not dishes?)

We are told, after all, that there are "many other things that Jesus did" (John 21:25) not recorded anywhere. The Gospels give us tantalizing glimpses of Jesus in heated discussion with both disciples and opponents, and these suggest that many challenges he uttered were followed by serious back-and-forth discussions of the kind I've imagined. At least that's the spirit of the man I encounter in the Gospel texts: strong in principle, compassionate in relationship, willing to discuss and debate, even when speaking words so challenging as to sound harsh.

Respect rules, but go beyond the rule-maker's way.

Do not think that I have come to abolish the law or the prophets; I have come not to abolish but to fulfill. . . . For I tell you, unless your righteousness exceeds that of the scribes and Pharisees, you will never enter the kingdom of heaven.

—Matthew 5:17, 20

And challenging words they are, even the ones that look easy on the surface. As we begin to explore a saying like "love your enemies" or "give to those who ask" or even "love your neighbor as yourself," we're likely to discover aspects of ourselves we've not encountered before and situations that demand good critical thinking about how to deal with complex realities. The rough edges of our souls will be revealed, as well as strengths we didn't imagine we had. We'll discover new confusions. Just how do I "love" a colleague who slurred my reputation to get the promotion that was mine? Or a neighbor who plays loud music late at night? Or my child who can't keep a job and wants to borrow money again?

With rules, you can "just do it." You really don't have to exceed the speed limit, walk on the grass, or use your cell phone at the movies. But "give to those who ask" is both a summons to generosity and a challenge to learn how to do it in ways that are truly blessings to others. You have to go beyond rule keeping into soul growing.

Jesus' sayings don't work very well as rules, and his biggest fights were with those who saw religion as rules rather than wisdom to grow souls strong. Rules apply specific principles like love and justice to particular situations. They can be kept externally, formally, without any change of heart or mind. The challenge embodied in a saying like "It is more blessed to give than to receive" (Acts 20:35) is more soul-penetrating than a prescriptive rule. Its life-shaping truth is slowly discovered only by the day-to-day experience of the practice.

Some people would disagree with me strongly, I know. Many Sunday school teachers and preachers would say my feeling of inadequacy in the dream was precisely correct, because Jesus' sayings are given to make clear how sinfully weak we actually are. We are meant to throw ourselves abjectly on the mercy of God, begging forgiveness for the sinfulness of our nature. But it seems to me any teacher who sets challenges before students in order to demonstrate the students can't accomplish them is a sadist or worse.

True, like a martial-arts master, Jesus provokes us not only to evoke our strengths but also to help us find our weaknesses and places of resistance. This is not so our faults can be judged harshly but so that God's grace can work with us, strengthening our weaknesses, shaping our whole self into a richer, fuller, stronger humanity—the capacities that make up the "image and likeness" of God in us.

Each of Jesus' sayings is an invitation to discover the muscles of our heart, mind, and soul—the movements of God's love made flesh, step-by-step, in our own lives. Jesus' challenge to Martha, for example, has more than once helped the Martha in me relax while hosting a gathering and pay loving attention to the people present rather than devote anxious concern to every detail of the party.

Rules may produce conformity, but challenges produce distinctive fruit in different lives and communities through time. Each person, each community, each era, is very particular soil that produces differing results. For example, giving alms to beggars on the street was appropriate for medieval Europe but may not be the only or best way to respond to Jesus' challenge to care for the poor in our own day.

Because people live in community, it is necessary in each age to debate and decide what specific codes, rules of life, or community regulations best incarnate Jesus' vision for our own day. But such rules are seldom absolute for all time. As Jesus demonstrated by his sabbath breaking and refusal to honor some ritual codes, law must change when love learns new lessons.[2]

If Jesus' call for change in a particular saying annoys, troubles, or baffles us—something like "Turn the other cheek"—we may have hit upon an aspect of our psyche that needs a bit of prodding. Annoyances and bafflements are often the outer ring of even deeper resistances to growth in grace—"hindrances to compassionate mind" as the Buddhists describe it. If we see annoyance as a call to deeper exploration, we may discover that there are many times when "turning the other cheek"—not responding with retaliation to an injury or insult—is not only the most practical action but a challenge to examine the roots of our own defensiveness.[3] Jesus goes behind mere rule to provoke the heart into greater self-awareness.

Jesus' disciples are often baffled or annoyed at what he says to them. Take the issue of divorce, for example. Jesus seems to tell them that divorce and remarriage is simply not possible because man and woman have become "one flesh." (See the discussion in Matt. 19:3-12.) Such a strict rule was taught in that day only by teachers of the Dead Sea Scroll community.[4] The majority of Jews followed Rabbi Hillel, who allowed divorce for a wide variety of reasons; a minority followed the stricter Rabbi Shammai, who allowed divorce only in the case of adultery.

Jesus throws down the gauntlet to his disciples: heal the "hardness of heart" that leads to divorce rather than sever what God has joined together. The rule-keepers stop reading the text there, because they've got a sure, certain, black-and-white commandment: no divorce. But if you keep on reading, you see the kind of conversation I've imagined between Jesus and Martha breaking out.

As the story continues, we see that the disciples are appalled at what seems such a harsh ruling. No exit from a bad match except lifelong celibacy? "Better then not to marry at all!" they mutter. Jesus presses them: celibacy's not so difficult as they think! There are people celibate from birth because of genital defect, those made "eunuchs" by others, and those who choose to be "eunuchs" or celibates for the sake of single-minded devotion to God (possibly a reference to those Dead Sea monks).

One can only imagine the expression on the faces of the disciples, most of them married men with families. They hadn't signed up for this! Whatever those faces conveyed, or whatever unrecorded dialogue filled the spaces between the lines of our New Testament story, Jesus ends the debate with a still greater surprise: this stringent challenge is not a rule for everyone: "Not everyone can accept this teaching, but only those to whom it is given."

What is "this teaching"? A rule for divorce? Or is it a challenge to deal with "the hardness of your hearts"? Jesus' summons is clear: God desires that marriage be a blessing, a place where hearts are transformed rather than hardened, where the difficulties that close the heart are dealt with before they kill the relationship. But the frailty of human nature is such that not everyone is able to do this heart-work equally well. Strong in principle, Jesus is compassionate in understanding the frailties of the flesh, acquainted as he is with his own through many struggles.[5]

The disciple community has been left to sort out the precise applications of this enigmatic teaching. The conversation is still going on, various sections of the Christian community coming up with different regulations about it.[6]

Why couldn't he have been clearer? I believe this is a deliberate technique. Like a Zen master, Jesus has pitched a real-life enigma into the disciple band to shatter the conventionality of their habitual thinking. Like Socrates and many rabbis in Jewish tradition, he makes his disciples struggle with difficult issues rather than giving them easy answers. Certainly few human realities are better suited to quandary than a troubled marriage! He goes beyond the rules about divorce to talk about hardness of heart, just as he goes behind the rule about adultery to pinpoint the lustful fantasies that lead to it, and inside the commandment against murder to force us to deal with the anger out of which murder comes. (See Matt. 5:21-28.) However we may deal with specific rules about marriage and divorce, we are bidden to cultivate a heart that can stay rooted in a desire for the well-being of the other in the midst of domestic strife, whether reconciliation or separation is the outcome. This is no easy task, but it is infinitely better than the bitter alternative.

There are many other enigmatic sayings in the Gospels, just lurking to trip up those looking for rule-bound consistency. Consider the famous response to the question about whether a good Jew should pay taxes to Caesar or not. "Render . . . to Caesar the things that are Caesar's, and to God the things that are God's," he says in easy-to-remember epigrammatic style (Matt. 22:21, NKJV).

The principle's clear enough: we have dual obligations, to the state and also to God. But Jesus doesn't tell us how this applies to any specific situation. We're supposed to wrestle hard in each time and place about how our obligations to God and to the state apply. The community of Jesus needs different rules in a Christian monarchy than in a pluralistic democracy or bloodthirsty tyranny. The rules change, but the principle remains a constant challenge.

A whole raft of such paradoxical brainteasers can truly baffle and annoy: inextricably linked opposites that declare seemingly conflicting values, each of which calls us to an important value or reality. "Look at all the works of the Most High," says a Jewish scripture popular in Jesus' day; "they come in pairs, one the opposite of the other" (Sirach 33:15). Or as a more famous passage suggests, love and hate are linked, as are embracing and refraining from embracing, mourning and dancing, tearing and sewing, war and peace (see Eccles. 3:1-8).

Jesus' teaching contains more than one pair of such opposites, though they are seldom reported side by side.

> Honor your father and mother. (Matt. 15:4)
> > vs. Hate father and mother. (Luke 14:26)
> Whoever is not with me is against me. (Matt. 12:30)
> > vs. Those who are not against us are for us. (Mark 9:40)
> Do not judge, so that you may not be judged. (Matt. 7:1)
> > vs. Judge with right judgment. (John 7:24)

The most dubious way to get clarity about these opposites is to rule one of them out of order. The usual tactic nowadays is to claim that he didn't say one or the other of them. But much of our life is spent reconciling opposites—boldness vs. caution, for example. And teaching in proverbial opposites is part of the folk wisdom through the ages. Ordinary proverbs and mottos advise us, paradoxically, to "look before you leap" while at the same time proclaiming "he who hesitates is lost." Opposites let us know the outer boundaries of our choices. Wisdom consists in knowing which applies when, and to what degree. No simple rule can substitute for the discoveries of real experience.

Follow me. Learn from me. Link yourself to the spirit of my words and deeds.

Come, follow me.
—MATTHEW 19:21

Take my yoke upon you, and learn from me.
—MATTHEW 11:29

Such inconclusiveness about the exact rules for all situations is enough to drive some people mad. Jesus, in fact, made the rule makers of his day wish to "destroy him" (see Mark 3:6). While some people seek security in religion, others seek the wisdom: real knowledge about how to live well. The Way of Jesus is for wisdom-seekers, people willing to risk the uncertainties of really learning how to serve the good in various situations, and in the process discovering where they need to grow. Playing it safe by rule-conformity alone can leave the heart unchanged, like a whitewashed tomb filled with dead bones (Matt. 23:27).

Jesus is looking for apprentices to this kind of wisdom. As Jews, Jesus' listeners recognized that he was creating an innovating, practical life–changing *halakah*, a way of responding to the commandments. *Halakah* is practical because it is, in fact, a set of *practices* intended to give flesh and bones to the written law. He called his Way of practicing Torah "my yoke" and invited listeners to become learners, who in turn taught others. Jewish prayers and writings make clear that "taking the yoke of the Kingdom" means practicing the moral and spiritual wisdom of the Torah. Much of Jesus' ethical teaching, in fact, is in line with the spirit of other rabbinical sayings of his day. But, unlike the burden of legalistically applied, rule-based perfectionism some of his contemporaries advocated, Jesus' yoke is "easy."[7]

A yoke seems, at first glance, to be a heavy load on the neck. But the symbolism of the double yoke is liberating rather than oppressive. Two oxen will be able to pull a cart or plow much more easily when linked together by the yoke because the yoke induces a synchronized walking that makes pulling a cart or a plow smoother and easier. Like its Sanskrit root word *yuj* (from which *yoga* also derives), the yoke means that two parties are linked together, in this instance: body and spirit, Jesus and his apprentices, humanity and God.[8]

I realized the truth of this metaphor vividly one sunny afternoon at a great seventeenth-century French estate when a friend and I took a rented swan boat out onto the reflecting pool. Two sets of pedals, like a bicycle's, propelled the small craft. For a few minutes my friend and I floundered about. Each of us pedaled to the best of our ability but got nowhere until we coordinated our rhythm. Our feet invisibly yoked together by cooperation, we sailed forward in the water with the elegance of the long-departed aristocrat who built the pond.

Like a swimming coach who invites us to join him in the water and start moving our muscles as he does, Jesus invites us to discover in our own experience how his sayings really bring forth the gold in human nature: "Test this teaching and know whether it's from God or whether I'm making it up" (John 7:17, THE MESSAGE).

Provoked to test and explore, our souls begin to be shaped into the practice of love, goodness, and justice God desires for human living. Even our mistakes can increase our emotional and spiritual wisdom. As we do this, we pass from an easy idealism to the chastening power of real life with all the confusions and revelations that actually alter our habitual behavior.

The overall goal is clear: participation in the compassionate love of God, by whose power we can love ourselves, others, and all of life with wisdom, skill, and grace. (See Luke 6:36.) Our task as apprentices is to become proficient, not perfect, increasingly skilled in graceful action rather than beyond any possible improvement. We are to become *teleioi*, "mature" or "developed" graduates in skill after skill for living. Such is the meaning of the word so often translated "perfect" in the Gospels (Matt. 5:48).[9]

One step at a time, we take Jesus' words into our souls and begin the process of letting them get to work on our lives. We need to ease ourselves into one challenge after another. As you go through this book—or skip around in it, according to your interest in various sayings of Jesus—here's a step-by-step way to deepen your apprenticeship, a way to cultivate the capacities of the heart.

QUESTIONS FOR REFLECTION AND DISCUSSION

1. Make a list of three or four sayings of Jesus that "call" to or provoke you through interest or annoyance—either ones in this book or others that haunt you from your reading of the Gospels.

2. Note which of these teachings most needs work in your life now. Don't bother with guilt about any failures. Just note that you're not very good at this right now and consider one of them your "cutting edge" practice for a stated period of time: a day, a week, a month, or longer.

3. List behaviors, actions, and attitudes that already embody this challenge in your life, however haltingly.

4. Brainstorm two or three ways this practice might improve your life and relationships. Then brainstorm two or three new ways to live it out. Pick one and start exploring ways to live it out.

5. Find some spiritual friends, fellow disciples with whom to share your discoveries and difficulties. Be part of a learning community in a local church or group of spiritual seekers.

6. Ask the Spirit that was in Jesus for help and guidance. Trust God to open opportunities for practice, and aim for lifelong learning!

The stories of Jesus' continuing presence after his death tell us, among other things, that Jesus has never stopped saying, "Follow me." As you read, be ready for the Voice that may speak through any of these chapters with the challenging invitation, "This I challenge you, now, in love, to do. See who you become as you do it."

CHAPTER 2

Transform Your Heart and Mind

JESUS INVITED PEOPLE then and now to see the world in a wholly new way, through different eyes: as the place where God's own powerful love for the world itself, for all that makes and keeps life holy, is meant to be the central passion of human life. As we let this love have its way with our personal and communal life, he said, we begin to enter, here and now on earth, the realm of God's active grace, what he called God's "kingdom" or "reign."[1]

The man from Nazareth saw earthly life with heaven's eyes, and he invites us to love each other, earth, and all earth's creatures with heaven's love, God's own just and merciful love. As we live into the love at the heart of Jesus' *halakah*, our actions more and more reveal that we are Wisdom's "children," offspring of the very Love that shaped the world and our deepest nature. (See Wisdom 7:22 and Luke 7:35.) Speaking in the ringing tones of the divine Wisdom that can make us "friends of God" (Wisdom 7:27), he reveals that at the heart of the ancient Torah, in the passion of the prophets and the proverbs of Israel's sages, breathes a love that longs to gather us together "as a hen gathers her brood under her wings" (Matt. 23:37) and teach us the "things that make for peace" (Luke 19:42).[2]

Jesus himself seems to have had a profound experience of that love at his baptism by John in the Jordan River, when he "saw"—presumably in a mystical vision—the heavens split open, was overshadowed by the mighty "wings" of God's presence, and heard a voice assuring him that he was deeply, utterly, totally loved: "You are my beloved Son; in you I delight" (Luke 3:22, REB).

From that moment on, this love was the driving force of his life and the center of his message. Rather than hugging that love to himself, he spent the rest of his short life giving it away to others, shedding love like sunshine, awakening others to their own identity as the beloved sons and daughters of God.

To speak of love can sound shallow and sentimental if we think that this power of the soul is simply a pleasant emotion rather than the "passion fierce as the grave," the "raging flame . . . strong as death" and "terrible as an army" of which the Scriptures speak. (See Song of Sol. 8:6; 6:4.) The love Jesus received and gave is not only warm and comforting but challenging and purifying, both food and medicine for the human heart, like the sunshine that both strengthens unfolding plants and destroys mildew. There is no wisdom without warnings, so Jesus, like the figure of holy Wisdom in Proverbs, not only invites us to learn the taste of love but its laws. He warns that there is no action without consequences, no growth without accountability. (See Proverbs 1:20-23.)

Transform your way of seeing.

Repent, for the kingdom of heaven has come near.
—MATTHEW 4:17

To see the world through the eyes of God's love, Jesus calls us to "go beyond our present state of mind"—the literal meaning of *metanoeite,* the Greek word ordinarily, and I think, unhelpfully, translated "repent."[3] This is literally the first challenge of the Good News, and all else follows from it.

Love is, at its core, our affirming response to the goodness of life itself, our *yes* to existence. This divinely sourced love, a reflection of God's own delighted declaration that the creation is "very good," is the flame at the core of our being, as near as the radiant smile evoked by a newborn baby or the emerging affection of a child for its parent. It fuels our friendships and helps keep us from letting our resentments and animosities run rampant through our relationships. It is the quiet basis for ordinary civility in which we treat others as we would ourselves be treated. In its more extraordinary forms, it drives forgiveness after deep injury, love for those quite different from us, fuels a passion for justice, and can even open our heart to the humanity of an enemy.

Such love is the capacity to see both the good and evil in people but to love the good; to see both the excellent and mediocre but to encourage the excellent; to see the wellness and the sickness and to strengthen the wellness. Before all else, love is the capacity to see everyone and everything as interconnected, "held together" in one cosmic embrace. (See Col. 1:17.)

I was given a glimpse of the nearness of this love in the dark days following the terrorist attacks on the World Trade Center, whose smoking ruins were quite visible from the mountain near my home in New Jersey. Awash with grief and fear, my wife and I had spent the day of the attack nervously awaiting word about neighbors and friends who worked in the Twin Towers. The ensuing days witnessed the intense sense of bonding with anyone and everyone in the community that sometimes emerges in times of crisis—people connected by the shared experience of vulnerability and loss.

Two days after the attack I went into the local supermarket, crowded at the predinner hour, and in the middle of sorting through apples found tears gathering in my eyes as a veritable rush of love moved through me. Everyone in the store seemed so beautiful, so incredibly alive, and so equally on the knife-edge of danger. I knew that they were all as rough-edged, imperfect, and sometimes downright ornery as I can be. A few were probably up to no good in some area of their lives. None of that mattered. We were all equally, utterly, completely, infinitely precious in the eyes of a Love clearly much bigger than I.

I dare to believe I was given a taste of the state of consciousness Jesus lived in habitually, a state reported through the ages by mystics and saints on every spiritual pathway. I understand more readily why Jesus challenges us to learn how to relate to everyone we meet in the light of what is revealed in such experiences, even if we don't feel such love at the moment.

Because behavior that crafts the soul toward ever fuller experiences of this love is so central to fully functional human life, Jesus makes it the central commandment or challenge of his message. The kingdom is made manifest among us by the embrace and enactment of this love, and we are bidden to make its learning the chief apprenticeship of our lives.

Learn how to love God, others, and yourself.

"You shall love the Lord your God with all your heart, and with all your soul, and with all your mind" . . . and . . . "your neighbor as yourself." On these two commandments hang all the law and the prophets.

—MATTHEW 22:37-40

"Thou shalt love" is a challenge—an invitation to discover by practice the central human capacity that makes all the rest worthwhile, a provocation that eventually surfaces all in us that hinders love. Love is not the only power of the psyche or soul to be cultivated, but it is the one meant to rule all the rest.

Love arises in us first as *eros*, the deep bonding we feel with some people from infancy onward, ranging from affectionate connection to sexual attraction. As necessary and God-given as this level of love may be, for some it remains the limit of love's reach. They love what pleases them and dislike what doesn't, period. Jesus calls us toward *agape*, a broader form of love that intentionally seeks the well-being of others simply because they are fellow creatures. *Agape* begins with the decision to do good regardless of feeling, but it can combine with empathy to create compassionate understanding, even of those we do not like.

Eros and *agape* are not totally separable, as we shall see. They show two faces of the same life-loving affirmation. *Eros*, which rises and falls as it pleases, needs *agape* to grow up out of mere selfishness. If we do not develop habits rooted in *agape*, even our erotically fueled relationships flounder, evaporate, or turn abusive. *Agape*, in turn, needs *eros* to keep its roots warm and moist.[4]

I was distressed to hear a preacher say recently, "Jesus delivers us out of law into love. You can't command or legislate love, for it comes from the heart and flows out spontaneously." He was not only confusing *agape* and *eros*, a common custom these days, but also pitting love against law as irreconcilable opposites rather than perceiving their inextricable link.

At its best, law describes what love does—those habits tested and proven to produce right relationships for people and societies. As Paul of Tarsus, himself a fierce opponent of legalistic moralizing, says, "Love is the fulfilling of the law" (Rom. 13:10).

Jesus interprets the commandments of the Torah as challenges aimed at cultivating *agape*, for this kind of love, unlike eros, can be commanded: "You shall! Learn how." A challenge to grow, step-by-step, invites us to discover muscles of the soul we may not realize exist.

Real love, whether *eros* or *agape*, is never self-evident, never fully proven by its proclamations or poetry. Real love is known by its deeds.

A few years ago, I had two graciously rude awakenings to this truth almost back-to-back in both my marriage and an important collegial relationship. My wife and I had recently witnessed a family blowup while spending a weekend with people I'll call Tom and Muriel. Tom had a temper that flared easily and inappropriately. His irritation at not being the center of Muriel's attention when others were around would build slowly, erupting eventually over some minor issue.

The morning after one of these temper tantrums, I saw the note he'd left out on the counter for his wife: "Really, really love you. Feel terrible. Sorry." I realized I was witness to a typical abusive pattern: annoyance, attack, remorse, good intentions, then repetition of the cycle. I suddenly recognized that "I love you" as impotent, captive to an abusive immaturity that broke the laws of love.

Not too many days later, Suzanne and I had a fight of our own. We both said outlandish things and hurt each other. As the storm passed, I heard with fresh ears my usual apology: "I really do love you, you know, in spite of what I said." Stunned into silence by the similarity of my protestation to Tom's note, I heard a voice inside me say, "Love is what love does. Nothing more. Nothing less."

My heart turned over—I know no other way to describe it; I realized that love in the heart is only half-real until it acts like love in actions. While reassuring my wife I feel love for her after speaking hateful words may be appropriate, my trespasses signal that my love still needs growing.

The cardinal or heart virtues—courage, self-control, justice, prudence (wisdom)—give love its walking legs and feet. We can describe, sometimes even legislate, what their behavior looks like. Without these virtues, love as either emotion or intention probably will prove ineffectual. We rightly expect from each other a pattern of behavior that builds up right relationship rather than trespassing against it. Paul, the earliest commentator on what Jesus meant by love, says that we know we've learned its ways when we are patient and kind; not envious or boastful, arrogant or rude, irritable or resentful. (See 1 Cor. 13:4-7.) Learning such love, the boastful and irritable Paul would be the first to admit, is a lifelong process.

Enter the kingdom now. Pay attention to what is before you in this moment.

The kingdom of God is not coming with things that can be observed; nor will they say, "Look here it is!" or "There it is!" For, in fact, the kingdom of God is among you.

—Luke 17:20-21

No one can see the kingdom of God without being born from above.... You must be born from above.

—John 3:3, 7

If you can see what is in front of you, all the mysteries will be revealed. . . . The kingdom is spread on the earth like grass, but you do not see it.

—Gospel of Thomas 5, 113, at

Jesus' command takes his apprentices into a training course in love, because love unfolds into all the specifics of the kingdom he sees dawning. Step-by-step, we work with God to make space on earth for God's own love and justice, welcome and pardon, outreach and healing, sacrifice and sharing to flow through human lives.

In contrast to other visionaries of his day, Jesus speaks about the kingdom of God in almost entirely *immediate* and *relational* terms. The others focus on coming events that will usher in the full power of God's reign on earth. A mighty warrior will arise to throw off the hated Roman yoke and end Israel's centuries of oppression. Or a semidivine angelic figure will descend from heaven in flames of apocalyptic vengeance, slay the world's wicked, grant immortality to the righteous, and restore the earth to paradisiacal splendor. People scrutinized the scriptures for the signs that would herald the hour of miraculous deliverance.

Jesus declares that the hour is now, the reign of God already active in our midst. The kingdom is happening now. People will not find the signs of the kingdom in the stars or obscure scriptural images but in lives touched by the healing, life-restoring power of God's love, available here and now. He tells the emissaries of John the Baptist who question his version of the kingdom: "The blind receive their sight, the lame walk, the lepers are cleansed, the deaf hear, the dead are raised, the poor have good news brought to them" (Luke 7:22).

While Jesus uses some of the apocalyptic imagery swirling through his society to indicate an even fuller manifestation of God's reign in the future, he pointedly directs the gaze of his disciples away from guessing games about future times to the spiritual potentials of the present moment. (See Acts 1:7-8.)[5] Acutely aware of his people's suffering, he nonetheless turns their minds away from armed revolt, warning that hating the enemy, hot-tempered clashes, and the looming rebellion were greater dangers than the oppression itself.[6]

Jesus' stories about the kingdom urge people to consider how the soil of their hearts receives the seed of God's word, how their hardness of heart may destroy relationships, why fullness of life flows from forgiveness, how being alert to the call of God at any hour is critical, how justice for the poor is required, and how social propriety and religious strictures may exclude people whom God's love would include. According to the Gospel of John, Jesus believed people could undergo a spiritual rebirth that allowed them to "see" the kingdom at work right now and live in it, even in a world filled with injustice, sorrow, and suffering (John 3:3).

Jesus' eyes are on neither a distant heaven nor a future cataclysm, but on what's right here in front of him, each day full of divinely given possibilities. As sayings from the extracanonical Gospel of Thomas put it, the kingdom is here among us, "spread on the earth like grass" if we but open our eyes to see what's right in front of our face.

Really seeing what was in front of him seems to have been important to Jesus. His keen eye saw the religious businessmen who cheated widows out of their meager savings and the attention-grabbing performance of some who led the prayers (Mark

12:40). He saw women who suffered the violence of male power misused (John 8:1-11) and took time with children whom his disciples thought were not worth his attention (Mark 10:13-16). His eyes followed the limp of the lame, the halting step of the blind and the shrouded faces of the leprous. (See Matt. 11:5.)

His gaze drank in the riotous color of the spring carpet of wildflowers in Galilee (Matt 6:28), noted the swoop of nearby birds, and did not turn away from the dead bird fallen by the side of the road (Luke 12:6-7). He beheld the unemployed workers hanging out in the town square (Matt. 20:1-3) and the tax collectors extorting unjust sums out of poor farmer's pockets (Mark 2:14-16). And to all these, his heart went out in compassion. As Matthew tells us about the crowds that followed him: "he had compassion for them, because they were . . . like sheep without a shepherd"(Matt. 9:36).

He saw the hidden potential in people: the rocklike leadership in the vacillating Peter and the moral sanity in the troubled Mary Magdalene (Matt. 16:18; John 1:42; Mark 16:9.) He even demonstrates a remarkable compassion for those who crucify him, his knowing eyes seeing behind their hatred a fear that keeps them from recognizing him or the injustice of their actions (Luke 23:34).

It's not all that easy to see what's in front of us. What we expect to see determines what data we let in. We often see the preconceptions in our mind rather than the reality. I witnessed a dramatic demonstration of this phenomenon one night in a Lenten class where we were practicing different kinds of meditation. We were practicing receptive attention to long stalks of field grass which each person held.

Instead of the rapt gaze everyone else was using, one man twirled the grass jauntily and smiled in secret amusement. As group members described "seeing" the grass, people waxed eloquent about their growing astonishment over the delicate beauty of what had seemed at first glance a homely weed. Finally the secret smile spoke: "I didn't have to do all that," he said proudly.

"I know this grass very well. I did my PhD thesis in biology on this species."

"Wonderful," I said, "but what about *this* stalk of grass? You've never seen it before." Well, yes, he had, he insisted—thousands of them. He knew every inch of it without looking at the grass. "But what about this particular break in that discoloration on this stalk?" I gently pressed.

No. Seen one, seen them all, he persisted. He knew too much about the grass to be able to see it, fresh and whole, with "beginner's mind," the receptive and inquiring gaze of the child Jesus urges us to adopt in order to enter the kingdom (Mark 10:15; Luke 18:17).[7] Others, happily, got the point, and probably never saw field grass the same way again.

While seeing field grass with eyes wide open may not be the most critical spiritual exercise, really seeing what's before you is crucial if God's love and justice are to have full sway in your life. One day on my way to a Chicago speaking engagement, I recognized how easy it is to be blind to the reign and call of God. Chatting amiably with my driver, I was startled when he suddenly braked, backed up, and leapt out of the car, running over to help an elderly man who had fallen on the sidewalk.

I realized, with some chagrin, that I also had registered the old man's fall but with very different eyes. My sensibilities were so dulled by life in the metropolitan New York area that I semiconsciously reacted, "What business is it of ours? Somebody else will help." I was asleep to the kingdom of God in our midst, dead to compassion's call. My driver's eyes, however, had seen with the light of heaven, and his response summoned me to stay more awake.

Such love grows gradually, through challenges that unmask our blindness and resistance. Beginning in our interactions with those closest to us, it grows strong by facing all that would hinder or undermine its full and complete reign in our lives.

QUESTIONS FOR REFLECTION AND DISCUSSION

1. What, in your experience, indicates God's love for the world? for human beings? for you?

2. In what ways have you experienced *metanoia*—"going beyond" your present state of mind—in your spiritual journey? How have you experienced seeing the world with new eyes?

3. Practice seeing a stalk of grass (or a flower or any object you wish) in the way described in this chapter. How does prolonged, loving, receptive attention to what is in front of you change the nature of what you see?

CHAPTER 3

Remove the Hindrances to Love

THE CAPACITY TO FEEL for the old man who stumbles and falls does not begin with an altruistic embrace of the world. When I stood in the supermarket and felt that rush of love for every living person, I had been prepared by all the loving relationships that preceded it. The love learned in personally affectionate relations is a foundational ingredient in the love Jesus talks about—a love that grows beyond such warm mutuality to face strangers and even, eventually, enemies with a compassionate gaze.

We learn to love because we are first loved. Most humans seem wired to find babies delightful. The evolutionary reason may be every infant's need to come into the world beheld in a burst of affection. That warm greeting is both a sign and an actual outreach of God's yes to the existence of each being.

We all need to experience, through other humans, a love that delights simply in our being. We are the "apple of the eye" to one or more persons, so much the object of special devotion that we are reflected in the "apple" or pupil of their eye. The first exchange of smiles between mother and child is a form of mutual provocation, a ritual initiation into a dance of receiving and giving that evokes those good feelings we usually call "love." This complex emotion arises in relationships where the exchange of words and deeds aimed at the good of the other fuels delight. Lack of that exchange stunts our growth into maturity.

This delight is meant to be the beginning of appreciative

inquiry into the world, eventually ending in our ability to see, with God, some glimpse of sacred humanity even in those who oppose us or hate us—a kinship that makes them also the children of God, however marred God's image may be in them.

Love one another from the heart.

Love your brother as the apple of your eye.
—GOSPEL OF THOMAS 25, AT

Love one another; as I have loved you.
—JOHN 13:34, NKJV

So much of Jesus' teaching is clearly about agape, the extension of goodwill to neighbors and even perfect strangers, that we may forget how necessary the health and well-being of our intimate loves is to the ability to open our hearts to the world beyond our immediate circle.

Compassion for those we do not love in a warm, connected way is, in part, an imaginative extension. We summon a bit of the empathy and understanding we have learned in close relationships to help us see the vulnerable humanity of a stranger, even one displaying off-putting behavior.

I sit stranded with dozens of others at Washington's Dulles International Airport, waiting for my much-delayed flight to depart. The man next to me jiggles his foot in frustration, an angry scowl on his face. He mutters curses about the airline and the hapless desk clerk stuck with the task of managing angry travelers. Since I can easily remember similar frustrations, I'm able to invite him to complain actively to me. I'm able to commiserate with him because others have commiserated with me. I know how important it is. He's still trapped but feels better and is less likely to badger the poor clerk. As people overhear, a conversational chain reaction starts in the waiting room. Soon lots of us are talking, empathizing with each other's plight, carrying the conversation to other topics. Community, however temporary, happens.

All this interplay is fueled by the ways each of us has learned to care about others' feelings in our more intimate experiences. Any attempt to love humanity at large by neglecting personal, particular love relationships is doomed either to failure or significant weakening.

Being deprived of affection in the early years stunts the growth of the human soul, perhaps even the development of the brain. The capacity for love remains undeveloped, a dry and unwatered seed in the soul, redeemable only by some later, virtually miraculous encounter with love.

I witnessed such a redemptive encounter in a recent television report. It documented the transformation wrought in hardened criminals by serving as hospice caregivers for other prisoners at Louisiana's Angola Penitentiary, the "biggest and baddest" maximum security prison in America. Louisiana law takes a dim view of letting murderers go free on parole, so most of those convicted end their days in jail. The new warden in Angola, a sincere Christian, felt that even murderers deserve to die with dignity, so he set up a hospice program. Rather than bring in volunteers from the outside as other prisons do, the warden invited prisoners themselves to do the job.

Those who responded to the request entered into a life-transforming practice that awakened love. One dying prisoner, a second-degree murderer in for life, said he'd spent his whole life getting "whatever you can take from somebody." "Then all of a sudden you find yourself getting something, giving something"—a great and unexpected blessing "because I ain't never known what that even meant."

Many such criminals come from families starkly void of any real caregiving. Early in life they learn that no one will care for them except themselves. Their stunted or stillborn capacity to love provides no balance or brake to the violence of which we all are capable. Few have known normal give-and-take, sharing, and the easy flow of mutual generosity.

Another dying prisoner speaking out of this deprived state

said, "why fellow inmates would look out and care for one another like they do" was simply beyond his experience. His caregiver, jailed for armed robbery, had "come up selfish, nobody," able to think only of himself. When he bathed his patient and received thanks for it, "it just did something to me." The latent, buried capacity for caring had been awakened, like the dawn of the baby's first smile.

By practicing the unfamiliar actions of loving care, the prisoners find their minds and hearts changing. They begin to see each other, however haltingly, through the eyes of a love they have never known before. As the prison chaplain puts it, "I have seen people here . . . become human beings. . . . people come here hardened or heartless, without feeling at all. Somewhere in the process, they open and change."[1]

The prisoners' experience demonstrates how love grows through actions as much as actions come out of love. It also underlines why Jesus envisioned the training for his apprentices necessarily taking place in groups of "brothers and sisters" rather than solely in solitary meditation and reflection. Being a disciple meant practicing love in the close quarters of a band of brothers and sisters who met together often enough to get past the first flush of comradely affection to the hard work of growing relationships that keep the affection alive.

And heart-affection it is. "Love your brother as the apple of your eye," just as we are loved by God (Ps. 17:8), Jesus says in the Gospel of Thomas. This saying, widely known in the early church, gives us a clue about his own way of growing in love. The canonical Gospels confirm that Jesus himself didn't just love disinterestedly but had at least two special friends who were loved deeply: the "beloved disciple," traditionally thought to be John, and Mary Magdalene, to whom the first vision of the Risen Christ came. The recently discovered Gospel of Mary has it that Mary was initiated into the band of the apostles and received Christ's kisses on her lips! That others now unknown caught his heart is indicated by his encounter with the rich young man who has set his heart on living out God's law: "Jesus, looking at him, loved him" (Mark 10:21). So also when Jesus wept at his friend Lazarus's tomb, the crowd murmured, "See how he loved him!" (John 11:36).

Such love, even the infatuation we call "falling in love," can on occasion help us to feel in love with the whole world, preparing our hearts for the deeper, more strongly muscled love that can seek justice, forgive hurts, pursue reconciliation, and remain steadfast in the face of opposition or evil. There is good reason why soldiers often keep the pictures of loved ones close to them in combat.

So start with those closest to you, Jesus seems to say, especially those with whom you share a common intent to walk the Way of Christ. Make the practice of love from the heart your aim.

Do not be angry with, insult, or despise your brother or sister.

I say to you that if you are angry with a brother or sister, you will be liable to judgment.

—MATTHEW 5:22

Practice, however, soon reveals the difficulties we face in learning how to love well. Very quickly love's course proceeds from delight to dismay. The nurturer may become the source of disappointment, even of pain. Our beloved, cooing, cradling adult puts us down and disappears, if only to sleep. Worse yet, the nurturer may become angry or annoyed. The lifelong task of dealing with disrupted relationships begins. If fortunate, a child begins to learn the disciplines that lead back to delight—all the arts of forgiveness and reconciliation, kindness, courtesy, and cultivating relationship that Jesus speaks of and embodies in his own life.

Social creatures like us cannot avoid experiences in which love is wounded, pride punctured, self-esteem threatened, and deeds misunderstood. Such experiences can kindle a hellish fire in our hearts that hinders love, closes us to relationships, or inspires us to seek revenge. For love to grow, all the wounds, grudges, and unforgiving resentments that would block its flow must be dealt with squarely as they arise.

While angry reactions are natural and inevitable, harbored anger corrodes the soul. Jewish tradition warns against such anger: "Do not get angry with your neighbor. . . . do not resort to acts of insolence . . . overlook faults" (Sirach 10:6; 28:7). Jesus warns against stewing in anger (Matt. 5:22). "Today's trouble is enough for today," he says, urging us to work for reconciliation immediately. (See Matt. 6:34; 5:23-24.) His invitation to "bless those who curse you, pray for those who abuse you" is wise advice for any disruption in relationship (Luke 6:28).

I see hurtful encounters quite differently when I imaginatively remember the scene bathed in the light of God's love. I'm likely to discover ways I contributed to the clash, even when I think the other person was mostly responsible. Most importantly, the practice of prayer for the offender helps free me from the emotional storm of my own anger.

My Christian practice has been enriched by practical Buddhist exercises that deal with the "poison" of anger. My Buddhist friend Robert John explains that these mind-shaping meditations do not seek "to eliminate but to transform" the energy of anger. The first step is to recognize that anger begins with the "delusion that we are in control of things." Anger is, in part, our surprised reaction when things don't go our way.

Why should we get angry when the toothpaste cap drops on the floor, be surprised when someone grabs the parking place we are aiming at, or even when someone hurts us? Habitual as our reaction is, it is rooted in a continuing refusal to recognize that we live in a world where such things—right or wrong—happen all the time. We can't control the flux, unpredictability, and impermanence of events, but we can cultivate a different reaction to them.

"If I am aware of my anger as it comes up," Robert John says, "observe it, and refrain from getting lost in mental judgments that spin the story of anger, I notice how anger is sheer energy: my body tingles, my heart beats faster, my breath gets short. Focusing on the sensations keeps me from spinning out into a mental soap opera of anger and injury, invites me to breathe deeply, and thus clears the mind to see some appropriate and nondestructive response. I drop the toothpaste cap. Rather than cursing either myself or the cap, I pick it up. The parking place is just there; it isn't necessarily 'mine.' I find another. I am better able to see how destructive anger is not only to others but to me. I can refrain from acting on it and find that with practice it subsides more quickly."

The parallel concept to this in Christian tradition is *detachment*—nonattachment to particular outcomes in events—which leads to *equanimity,* the ability to "roll with the punches." Cultivating such equanimity is intended, in both Buddhist and Christian practice, to clear mind and heart for compassion. What's driving that woman to snatch the parking place I had prior claim to? Anxiety? A family crisis? Just plain selfishness? Any one of these imagined possibilities is a doorway into some compassion for another soul who may be driven by heart-restricting feelings.

Do not use judgments to close your heart to love.

Do not judge, and you will not be judged.
—LUKE 6:37

Judge with right judgment.
—JOHN 7:24

Getting lost in tightly held judgments is destructive to love. On this point Jesus' teaching seems, at first glance, contradictory. He warns us not to judge others but seems perfectly capable of delivering finely honed judgments about people. In fact, he urges us to "judge with right judgment." Is this one of those paradoxical pairs?

Marianna had struggled with this since she was a teenager. She took very seriously Jesus' commandment not to judge but was defeated by a difficult brother-in-law. "No matter how hard I tried to treat him courteously, to reach out with acts of love, his rude, inconsiderate behavior and sarcastic wounding remarks never stopped.

"After many years, I found myself at the end of my rope," she told me. "Nothing I did made any significant difference." Friends who knew the family had exactly the same experience with a man apparently so lost in his own feelings he couldn't see clearly the reality of other people.

"Finally one day my son had come to the end of his patience with my stewing about this difficult relative. He said, 'Mother, Uncle George is just plain whacko. Why don't you just accept that fact? Jesus also told you not to cast your pearls before swine, didn't he? Give it up!'" Marianna saw more clearly than ever that he was right and that striving to change the situation was just driving her crazy. "But it all still felt terribly judgmental."

Marianna brought her quandary to a friend. "Isn't calling George a 'whacko' judgmental?" she asked. Her friend laughed. "I'd rather call it an astute assessment of the situation," he said. "Your brother-in-law sounds like a seriously limited man, with no idea of how he tramples on love offered."

Marianna's friend, a piano teacher to young children, went on to make the distinction clearer: "If I tell a student that she's playing the wrong notes and needs to practice more, that's an evaluation, an accurate assessment of her performance. Not to correct her would be a failure in teaching her the skill. But if I tell her that she's a lousy student or label her as stupid, that's a judgment in the sense that Jesus meant."

That distinction is true to the Gospel. In the section on anger, Jesus says that the judgment we must not render is *Raca*—calling another human being a worthless, wicked, unredeemable person. Such judgment belongs to God alone, who sees the heart. We're overstepping the boundaries when we simply discard people from any further care or consideration with contempt or vilify them with pejorative labels. Such judgments shrivel our own hearts and close the door to the future.

Marianna had, indeed, spent her energy futilely in a lost cause, in part because she confused assessment with judgmentalism. What loving stance toward the brother-in-law might be possible? "First, give up the hope that your loving behavior will be answered in kind," her friend said. "Second, recognize you're dealing with an emotionally disabled person, so be kind and behave courteously. Third, as the old saying goes, 'Leave him to heaven.' If you can find it in your heart, pray that someday, somehow, he's led out of the prison he's trapped in. See if, in your prayer, you can see aspects of the image of God in him still alive."

"Finally," her friend said, "give all that love you've poured out at him to someone else who can use it better." In fact, released from focus on this difficult relationship, she has time for deeper friendships with other people, a closer relationship with other relatives, and unimpeded energy for her community service.

Forgive those who trespass against you.

Forgive and you will be forgiven.
—LUKE 6:37

Why do you magnify your brother's or sister's fault and ignore your own?
—MATTHEW 7:3, AT

If you loose the sins of any, they are loosed; if you retain the sins of any, they are retained.
—JOHN 20:23, AT

"There are deeds that are inexcusable, but no person is unforgivable," my surprised mind heard my mouth saying. A businessman I'll call Frank had just asked, "How can Jesus expect me to forgive my business partner? He ruined the business. His behavior was dishonest, destructive, and inexcusable."

Frank had grown up feeling forgiveness means allowing inexcusable behavior to be overlooked or excused without accountability. Whether my response came from the back of my mind or the Spirit's prompting I'll never know, but it answered Frank's question and clarified the meaning of forgiveness for me: Forgiveness is about the relationship, not about the deeds. It is the willingness to stay in relationship, even relationship significantly altered by trespasses, rather than closing the door for all time. Holding people accountable to make amends does not contradict the spirit of forgiveness. And even after forgiveness, all concerned may have to live with the ongoing consequences of the trespass.

"Forgiveness is neither amnesty not amnesia," says my friend Kay, a hospital chaplain. "It isn't that you forget the deed or that the other person doesn't need to make amends. Forgiveness is what makes that further work possible. Forgiveness is a gift for the sake of the relationship." As Archbishop Desmond Tutu, who has known and suffered many inexcusable actions as a South African black man, says: "There is no future without forgiveness."[2]

Don't let wounds fester, Jesus tells us: When we remember that our brother or sister has something against us, we are to go to him or her and be reconciled without delay. (See Matt. 5:23-24.) If someone has offended us, Jesus lays out a procedure: speak to the person privately, without delay. If this does not bring about reconciliation, bring in others to help both of you. Don't let the relationship lapse unless the other person absolutely refuses reconciliation. (See Matt. 18:15-17.)

I know a family in which two sisters were divided for decades over the distribution of family heirlooms after the death of their mother. Such family fights over heirlooms are, sadly, quite common. The sister I'll call Madge, swamped with the care of young children, left it to the older brother I'll call Lloyd to make the final judgments. After the division of antique quilts and Victorian furniture, Madge felt cheated and turned a cold shoulder to her brother who claimed items to which Madge felt entitled. Madge shared her resentment with her children, who carried the cold shoulder into the next generation, even after their mother's death.

Finally, one of Madge's children, rounding forty, decided all the relatives were just hurting themselves by holding onto resentments long since gone cold and meaningless, and she reached out to her aging Uncle Lloyd. As they talked about the estrangement, the complexity of the original situation emerged in its ambiguities and contradictions.

Misunderstandings had arisen on both sides. Lloyd had misunderstood a hasty phone call from his busy sister and divided items differently than Madge had requested. Silent estrangement ensued and persisted. An heirloom rocker and an ancestral quilt may be precious, but they are hardly worth thirty years of alienation. What a loss this family had suffered!

The reconciliation was relatively simple once the situation was actually addressed. Serious injuries are harder. *Reconciliation* after injury cannot happen without remorse, repentance, and change of behavior in the offender, and Jesus tells us to extend it to people when they ask forgiveness (Matt. 18:21-22). But *releasing* the burden of resentment in advance can prepare the way. A priest friend told me about preparing a sermon on the scene in the Gospel of John (20:10-23) when Jesus gives his disciples the power to "loose" (or "remit") the sins of others or "retain" (or "bind") them. On this occasion, the priest saw the words from a completely new angle. "I realized that when I 'loose' those sins, my own heart is 'loosed' from the power of brooding on the injury. If I 'retain' those sins, I'm still carrying them. I don't want that burden, so forgiveness frees my heart to live more deeply"—and actually be healthier, according to some heart specialists.[3]

The process of working to forgive injuries also helps us see more clearly the common humanity we share with those who have injured us. Basically, Marianna hadn't been able to forgive her brother-in-law for being who he was. Lack of forgiveness usually begins with refusal to accept one or more key facts in the situation, beginning with the obvious fact that all human beings are imperfect, fallible, and capable of downright wretched behavior. Granted these facts, all human beings have multiple occasions to practice forgiveness.

I harbored a resentment against a friend for an unkind act for many years, even as she reached out to restore the friendship. Outward forms were put in place again, but my heart remained closed. Then one day, as I got stuck on "forgive us our trespasses" in the Lord's Prayer, my closed-hearted condition filled my mind. Into this tightly locked mental space came a memory of myself doing something similar to someone else, and I was suddenly helplessly exposed as excusing myself while holding my friend to the standard I myself had violated. In a quiet rush, the cold resentment simply drained out of me. I had been "magnifying my sisters's fault" and ignoring my own. Our old relationship cannot be recaptured, but I've begun to cultivate a new one.

Jesus makes forgiveness a centerpiece of his teaching because lack of it lies at the root of so much human misery. The resentment that festers in unforgiveness and the misunderstandings that multiply in estrangement fuel most forms of personal and social conflict. Jesus calls humanity to face a stark truth: You cannot receive forgiveness if you do not give it. This is not some legalistic requirement but a realistic statement of the human psyche's emotional dynamics. God's forgiveness can't flow to or through closed, unforgiving hearts.

God's reign will be fully implemented when forgiveness has taught us where our best interests lie, for forgiveness is a basic form of self-interest. It may seem far-fetched to see forgiveness as key to the eventual success of the human venture on this planet, but forgiveness, followed by reparation and change, may be the ingredient without which no other element can finally succeed. Friendships and marriages fail because one party can't forgive the other. Political parties slide into vicious fights in which injuries sustained from mean-spirited power plays damage the common good. Ethnic conflicts smolder for generations. If Palestinians and Israelis, for instance, never forgive each other, in spite of all the injustices on both sides of their seventy-five-year-old conflict, what future have they?[4] The United States, in effect, forgave Germany by rebuilding the country after World War II, while still holding war criminals accountable for their inexcusable deeds.

The heart closed to giving forgiveness makes itself too small to cope with the inevitable injuries of life. It blocks the Love that would turn us away from the ways we undermine our best interests and turn us to "the things that make for peace" (Luke 19:42) between individuals and warring groups.

QUESTIONS FOR REFLECTION AND DISCUSSION

1. Practice remembering hurtful encounters "in light of God's love." As you re-imagine the scene, let a divine Light literally bathe everyone involved. Be open to new insights about all involved. Imagine how you might have acted differently. What do you see?

2. What's the difference between judgmentalism and right judgment? How could this distinction help you in dealing with others?

3. Remember an instance when you've been able to forgive. What inner process did you go through to reach the place of forgiveness?

CHAPTER 4

Put God's Priorities First

WHAT GOD LOVES is good for the world. The Divine Love, because it delights in all that creates good for all earth's creatures, has definite preferences and priorities. While it understands and seeks to heal the dark roots of resistance out of which destructive behavior grows, this Love sets its face against all that despoils and destroys the goodness of life.

Jesus calls us to put what God loves first: "Strive first for the kingdom of God." If we put what God loves first, everything else falls into its proper order of importance. It's that simple and that provocative, for it challenges any lesser priority.

Humanity's sorrows arise when retaliation and revenge rule; when grudges and hard-heartedness hinder reconciliation; when refusal to share dominates public and private life; when billions live in want while a minority feasts; when lack of restraint ravages earth's very fabric. To proclaim love the antidote for these ills seems foolish only if we forget that love—love of reconciliation over retaliation, cooperation over conflict—provides the fire for the tough and persistent patience, justice, courage, self-control, and wisdom required to preserve and develop all that is good. What other remedy for the ills of human life is there?

Seek the divine desire first in all things.

Strive first for the kingdom of God and his righteousness, and all these things will be given to you as well.

—MATTHEW 6:33

"Put God's desires first, and your deepest desires for a good life will come true," Jesus says. If he were talking to daffodils about the priority of sunlight or telling fish that passing water through their gills is necessary for anything else to be possible, there might be no danger of misunderstanding. But he's talking to human beings, who tend to see life in either/or categories: either God or the world, God or my career, God or my own happiness. So it's easy to mistake his meaning, as if God's desires were somehow automatically the opposite of our deepest desires rather than the fulfillment of them.

When in my ardent teenage piety I told an agnostic friend that God had to come first in my life, he said, "Even before your wife when you get married?" Oh, yes, I fervently assured him, God comes first. "You'll have a bit of difficulty finding any woman who'll put up with that," he told me with some scorn.

I had been raised to believe God's desires and mine were polar opposites. And who could blame me? Preachers for centuries have used Gospel passages that seem to suggest an either/or choice between God and every creature on earth.

Such pious paroxysms came to a head one evening in seminary as my heart soared to the heartrending beauty of a Bach harpsichord concerto—a secular, not a sacred, piece. I fell from beauty into pious worry: would love of such earthly beauty distract me from love of God? Ambivalence stewed in me until the next day, when it leaked out in a reflection paper I had written for my seminary tutor. A great fan of Bach himself, my tutor smiled and said quite simply, "But isn't beauty itself a manifestation of God in the world? Can't you love God in Bach's music, through God's music?"

This perspective was new to me. I imbibed it as saving grace. The seminary chaplain sealed this new realization later that year by proclaiming that "God dwells at the heart of everything in the world." It became clear for the first time that I could love God as beauty through all that is beautiful. Putting God's priorities first means loving the good in everyone we meet and everything we see and handle—a far cry from the world-shunning piety of my childhood training.

I'm fortunate to have perceived this truth before I met the woman who would become my wife. Suzanne would never have put up with my either/or approach to the God/wife issue for a minute. She already knew better than I did that the love of God is manifested in how we treat the world and each other: "If we love one another, God lives in us" (1 John 4:12).

Any long-term relationship, and most especially marriage, is a crucible in which desires are sorted out. Which will we give the highest priority? I could love my wife out of the most greedy level of personal desire: get me food now, make me comfortable now, agree with me all the time, make love to me when I want to, support me uncritically, and don't get too feisty. Some needy and immature part of me has felt every one of those desires at some moment in the last thirty-five years. She, too, has her own jumble of greedy desires.

With a bit more maturity, thank God, I've learned to love my wife for herself rather than her convenience to me: her own personal qualities of compassion and generosity, intelligence and ingenuity. The more we can see each other clearly, rather than through the lens of our own needy cravings, the more we are able to love, respond to, and encourage the good in each other. At moments, we can feel a love greater than our own flowing through us to each other. We have been prepared for those moments by repeated decisions not to be ruled by the less mature forms of our love. Firm, sometimes difficult choices must be made in order to follow the highest good in given situations.

For example, Suzanne loved me enough during a struggle with depression to overrule my wishes for isolation and call friends in to help. In that act she was loving Christ more than her husband—for the sake of her husband. To follow the good, she had to summon courage to override her own doubts and the fear I would feel betrayed. She chose God's priorities for her husband's well-being rather than his fearful requests.

Serve only one master: you can't serve both God and money.

You cannot serve God and wealth.
—LUKE 16:13

Do not store up for yourselves treasures on earth, ... but store up for yourselves treasures in heaven.
—MATTHEW 6:19-20

Love and money go together. The God Jesus knew cares a lot about money and how we use it, because what we love determines how we spend our money. How we spend our money, in turn, helps create our own personal world and affects the world at large. So it's not surprising Jesus gives us forthright challenges about God's priorities for our money. Following the prophets before him, he has a great deal to say about the power of money to corrupt or bless human life.[1]

Don't treasure money, Jesus commands. Treasure instead the good you can do with it: "for where your treasure is, there your heart will be also" (Luke 12:34). Easier said than done, which is why he warns us that we cannot "serve God and wealth" at the same time. You will either treasure the good or make money into a good all by itself, hug it to your heart, and use it to pander to your cravings. Like a drug.

Money as much as liquor makes people high and can impart a false sense of security. One drink may indeed fortify your nerves. But too many drinks will undermine your native powers. Every major spiritual tradition warns that lust for money can undermine the human spirit. Money is power, usable for greater or lesser purposes—a dangerous power unless brought under the governance of a still higher power, the compassionate love and justice of God.

In the Hebrew Bible, the capacity to accumulate wealth was regarded as the generosity of a bountiful God, to be used by king and commoner alike for the common good, not just for one's own pleasure or security. Alms for the poor and the justice of the king help maintain society's well-being.[2]

Jesus doesn't lay down a blanket rule that you can't accumulate money. Some of his disciples were part of family businesses that apparently continued to operate during his ministry (Mark 1:20).[3] Jesus himself owned or rented a house in Capernaum, had enough to give money to the poor, and was leading an evangelistic campaign that took donations and had a treasurer. (See Mark 9:33; 10:10; John 13:29.) Only a few people are ordered to give up their wealth: Matthew the tax collector, whose fortune comes by taking far more from the poor than the prescribed tax, and the rich young ruler whose attachment to his possessions may have been a solid barrier to trusting God. Most people are to use money not only to meet legitimate needs but to do real good: "Give to those in need" (Matt. 5:42, NLT). Like so many of Jesus' teachings, this one puts us squarely into a push-pull situation between all the cravings money can arouse in us and God's desires for money to be a blessing, not a curse, for us and for the world.

A young man I'll call Jim is an ardent Christian, deeply committed to Jesus' ethic of radical sharing and service to the world's needs. Jim shared freely with his friends and tithed to church and charity. But as his income began to rise, he says, "I began to feel a desire to cut back on giving money. Hey, those accumulating thousands of dollars in the savings account feel pretty good. Seems like the more I have, the less I want to part with it."

Part of Jim's pleasure in his growing bank account derives from justifiable pride in accomplishments and a reasonable sense of security for future family life. But he faces a spiritual test in deciding how to deal with his reluctance to part with a portion of that symbolic security. Will his heart choose to trust in riches or be "rich toward God" in good stewardship of his growing prosperity?

I know how Jim feels. When I took a 50 percent reduction in

income to follow the call to educational ministry, fears about financial insecurity rose to the surface. While my wife and I had enough to make ends meet, those first few years of financial struggle taught me two things: the value of each dollar and the fact that others have less than I do.

Exquisitely aware of money issues, we were appalled when my wife learned she needed two crowns put on her teeth. How could we afford them? Only the generosity of our dentist, who allowed time payments, saved the day. As marginal as we felt, we were still better off than people who lived in nearby, poorer neighborhoods. Our marginal financial situation led to a realization: what do really poor people do when a tooth breaks? Much to our own surprise, this realization led us for the first time to practice real tithing, even on a more limited income. We earmarked part of our tithe for the poor because as recipients of generosity, we felt called to pass it on.

Jesus challenges us to store up "treasure in heaven"—a phrase drawn from the rabbinical idea that charity for the poor is an investment in heavenly treasure—rather than hoarding treasure on earth.[4] Jesus called people to this compassionate sense of community where rich and poor are not divided into separate, isolated camps. He gathers a community that relies on just and loving relationship as its basis of fellowship, not status and power. Rich and poor alike are welcome in Jesus' fellowship, but all are called to devote their energy and goods to the common good.

I know wealthy people who, perhaps like the rich young man, live in fear of losing their money; no amount would ever be enough. I know others with even more, who are, in the old phrase, "open-handed" in their generosity, because they follow the call of a deeper and healthier part of their heart—a heart that shares God's priorities for the world. As I have suggested in other writings, we need to see all our assets as a joint account we hold together with God, to be spent to love God, others, and ourselves in appropriate order.[5]

Certainly the couple in my first parish, not wealthy but well-off, who supported my desire to return to graduate school with a gift of a year's tuition and the loan of an old car were not storing up riches for themselves. When I offered to pay the money back over time, they said, "No. Do something for someone else some day."

They were passing on blessings they themselves had received, as does an affluent couple, true "compassionate conservatives" who tackle a major charity project in each city they move to, sustaining an inner-city choir here, a poor student in a private school there. Their identity is tied up not with what they possess but with what they can do with it for God's purposes.

Let go of your defended self-image and find a truer self in God.

Those who want to save their life will lose it, and those who lose their life for my sake will find it.

—MATTHEW 16:25

If we follow Jesus' provocation to grow beyond our present state of maturity, we'll find not only our social roles but our very self-image challenged. Jesus' challenge to "lose your life" in order to find it does not require that we deny who we essentially are but invites us to discover our deepest and truest selves. Only God knows the secret of that self, but we find it through the years by putting God's priorities first in our lives, challenging the fears and resistances that keep us from growing. Don't hold on tight to your identity, your life, or your psyche, says Jesus.[6] Be willing to let go of the current boundaries of your identity for the sake of responding to God's call.

As a child, the slave Frederick Douglass followed an inner call to learn how to read. Even though it was against the law in Maryland, blacks being imagined inferior, his owner's wife, charmed by the boy, taught him until her husband discovered the clandestine meetings. As the man raged at his wife, the young Douglass realized with astonishment that the white slave owner knew very well blacks were capable of reading and feared his learning the skill. Simultaneously, Douglass felt the silent voice of God disclosing to him that he was capable, worthwhile—the equal of the white man. He let go, once and for all, of his slave identity, even though he continued in outward captivity for some years.[7]

Through the centuries God's call has liberated people to find their truer selves: the stuttering Moses finds his voice as the prophet of God; the prince Siddhartha breaks out of the protected pleasures of his father's palace, finds compassion for those who suffer, and thus becomes a Buddha; the dandy Francis of Assisi sheds his finery to live a life of solidarity with the poor; the slave trader John Newton becomes an abolitionist; the ex-slave Harriet Tubman discovers the strength to shepherd escaped slaves along the underground railroad; the musician Albert Schweitzer gives up his budding concert career to deliver medical care to the needy of Africa. These examples illustrate not just changes of behavior; they demonstrate new aspects of the self coming to the forefront, with struggles, doubts, and resistances we can only imagine.

A woman whom I'll call Carolyn had no idea she harbored a gift of spiritual healing until her husband challenged her to use it consciously. He suffered from chronic, low-grade depression and began to notice how her touch made him feel better. At first he thought he was simply reacting emotionally to her caring, but he began to notice that his energy seemed stronger from her embrace. One morning, after they had shared their morning devotions together, he felt moved to say to her, "I think you have a gift of healing, and I think it could really help me."

Carolyn's self-image had no room for this idea. She was the last person she would imagine to have such a spiritual gift. Still, at her husband's prodding, she agreed to put her hands on him and pray. "What do I do?" she asked. "I don't know," was the response. "Just open yourself to God and see what happens." As she did, she began to feel a subtle current of energy moving through her. He felt the energy coming into his cold and sluggish body, buoying up his spirits and stimulating his own energy.

After a long "treatment," Carolyn's husband felt better than in many days, but Carolyn felt her own resistances and doubts powerfully aroused. Was this real? If it was, what would she be required to do? How could she, of all people, have a gift like this? Her whole sense of self was as a much more "ordinary" person. But because her husband benefited from her laying-on-of-hands, she persisted and gradually came to claim the gift, and with it a new sense of her own giftedness. She has never felt called to declare her gift in public but uses it quietly with people who cross her path.

The world is filled with tales of ability discovered and used, as well as the untold stories of people who, holding tightly to their smaller selves, resist recognizing talents that could aid God's purposes in the world.

My smaller self was, I discovered, all too comfortable in the role of a clergyman. Until I found my ministry taking me beyond the walls of the parish, I didn't realize what a powerful hold the clergy role had on me. After a rewarding thirteen years in congregational ministry, I felt strongly called to the ministry mentioned above—community-based teaching in an interfaith and often secular setting. I didn't anticipate the resistances this call would set off in me.

The parish offered the security of a familiar group of people week by week, whereas my new work in one-time workshops presented me with many strangers. How different this experience was from the deference almost automatically conferred on me as a collar-clad priest! More than I realized, part of me had been "coasting" in the security of my role. Now my very anxiety forced me to grow. My presentation skills improved. I faced down my unexpected insecurity in standing before unfamiliar groups of people. My heretofore muffled fear of criticism and even failure was trotted out before me to be confronted head-on. I became more whole as a person, less dependent on the clergy role to do a ministry that took me progressively deeper into the public life of my community. Following the call, I found a deeper security in God and a deeper acquaintance with my own abilities.

The Divine Love knows what people need and what the world needs. The selves that emerge from responding courageously to such challenges are far richer than any we might invent for ourselves.

QUESTIONS FOR REFLECTION AND DISCUSSION

1. Do human desires and God's will always conflict? Make a list of two, three, or more of your deepest desires. Make a separate list of at least six desires you believe God has for human well-being. Now compare the two lists. In what ways might your own deep desires be aligned with God's desires—or become more aligned?

2. Review your own budget priorities in the light of God's desires. How much or how little are your monetary decisions serving or resisting God's desires for human well-being as you understand them?

3. In what ways might God be calling you into a "bigger self," calling you to love qualities in your makeup you may underestimate?

CHAPTER 5

Practice God's Family Values

DECISIVE ACTION IS sometimes required to love the good and turn away from any lesser allegiance that threatens it.

"Alice" realized she was a quiet alcoholic: "not a drunk—just well-oiled every evening." Disliking the personality changes her nightly cocktails produced, she stopped cold. As she awoke from this alcoholic "numbing," dormant feelings emerged. She began to attend personal growth seminars, became more involved in community activities, and gathered a whole new group of friends who supported her growth. She blossomed.

Her blossoming provoked her husband's resistance. He had rather liked the tranquilized person he found at home each evening and was less pleased with the vivid woman who now greeted him. He criticized her new friends, complained about her new activities, and denied she had a drinking problem. Repeatedly he offered her wine at dinner. She refused, persisting in her sobriety. Supported by her new "family," Alice grew spiritually in ways she'd never imagined, and her husband received the gift of a more loving, if more independent, wife. Eventually he came to appreciate the energetic and colorful new spouse in his life much more than the old, quiet, manageable one.

Don't let your ultimate loyalty be to family, clan, or tribe.

Whoever . . . does not hate father and mother, wife and children, brothers and sisters, . . . cannot be my disciple.
—LUKE 14:26

"Honor your father and mother."
—MARK 10:19

Jesus says a great deal about where the family stands in God's priorities, little of which makes him an ideal poster child for what some people think of as "family values." For example, he tells us to "hate" our family—the whole interlocking clan: siblings, spouse, children, parents. On the other hand, he affirms the commandment to "honor your father and mother."[1]

We're faced with yet another of those paradoxes. In what sense are we to "love" and to "hate"?

We are called to love the God-created good in everything. To do this sometimes requires choices that reject the "world" conjured by the baser desires of the human mind—in Alice's case, her husband's desire for control, security, and comfort. Jesus calls people to renounce that world with an aversion of the heart so decisive Jesus calls it "hatred." (See John 12:25.)[2] This hate is not the smoldering, resentful emotion that usually leaps to mind upon hearing the word. Rather, this aversion of the heart forcefully refuses all that would spoil what is best for human beings. Such aversion is sometimes necessary to jolt us out of the fantasy world of our cravings into the world of real people, things, and creatures we are called to love. Breaking our attachment to lesser things often takes an emotional force as strong as hate in this sense.

By decisively rejecting her husband's greedy desires for her, Alice "hated" her spouse and "honored" her family simultaneously. Jesus' use of "hate" shocks us in our own time, but in his day such a challenge to family and clan power was virtually blasphemous. His own behavior to his family was cause for considerable alarm.

"Child, why have you treated us like this?" asks his mother after she and Joseph have sought their son "in great anxiety" for three days after the Passover festival in Jerusalem. When they find him in the Temple courtyard engrossed in Torah discussions with older men, Mary says (in what tone of voice we can only imagine), "Look, your father and I have been searching for you in great anxiety." (See Luke 2:41-50.)

It is hard for us to hear the shocking discourtesy in Jesus' response: "Didn't you know that I must be in my Father's house, about his business?" The boy, not so subtly, has just discounted Joseph's authority as father in a time when fathers expected subservient behavior and deferential speech. Blatant pursuit of one's personal whim was deeply disrespectful. The text is at pains to reassure us that, after this breach, Jesus "was subject to them" (Luke 2:51, NKJV)—but only for the time being.

An open break with the family seems to occur after Jesus' mystical experience when the divine voice declares him "Beloved Son" at his baptism. Confirmed in an identity deeper than family or clan, his preaching and teaching draws great crowds. As word spreads like wildfire, his family hears of his activity and goes out "to restrain him, for people were saying, 'He has gone out of his mind'" (Mark 3:21).

Are family members concerned about Jesus' reputation—or perhaps their own? Do they themselves think he is insane? Or do they feel he's going about his "Father's business" the wrong way? Certainly John the Baptist felt Jesus was on the wrong track. (See Luke 7:18-23.) If the family is, as Luke depicts it, among those radical, antiestablishment Jews who were looking "for the redemption of Jerusalem" (Luke 2:38), they too may deem Jesus' mission strategy wrong-headed, too pastoral, too welcoming of the disreputable, too lacking in John the Baptist's fiery condemnations.[3]

The family's harsh judgment is soon met by Jesus' strong words. When they show up to take the family "crazy" home, Jesus declares that his "real" mother, brothers, and sisters are not blood relatives but "whoever does the will of God." (See Mark 3:21-35.) If Mary and the brothers want to be part of Jesus' family, they need to respect his call from God. As the story goes, the family, put in their place, did eventually come around to adopting Jesus' priorities, were present in the aftermath to the crucifixion, and became an important part of the early Christian community.

Parents stand for the transmission of values between generations. They, along with the other "parents" of society—teachers, mentors, and public figures—mold the expectations, desires, and behavior of children, and rightly so. But children can too easily be seen as extensions of the parental psyche, captive to desires that do not serve the real good of the child. I've met parents who are determined that their child will attend the same university they did, whether it is the best place for them or not. There are grandparents who withhold educational funds from grandchildren because they choose music rather than medicine, computers rather than corporate law. And there are families who try to control children through guilt and shame because the children seek more life-giving values than they have found at home. Even families who think they want the best for their children often pressure them into activities and values that may not serve their real talents and soul-needs.

Jesus' challenge to the family summons parents and spouses to embody a love that transcends and transforms any family agenda smaller than God's own love for people and the world. When children are brought to me for infant baptism, I try to put Jesus' challenge in a simple way: "By baptism, we're giving this child a new last name—Christ. Your family name becomes one of this baby's middle names. From now on, this is Katie Christ, and our job as family and community is to help this child grow up to love what God loves."

Love your family as Christ loves them.

**Whoever . . . does not *hate* his father and mother . . .
cannot become my disciple. Whoever does not *love* his
father and mother as I do cannot become my disciple.**
—GOSPEL OF THOMAS 101, AT, emphasis added

Call no one your father on earth.
—MATTHEW 23:9

The paradoxical linking of "love" and "hate" for family sets
up two values that need to find a right balance in each new situation. When Jesus advises us to "call no one father on earth,"
the challenge involves figuring out how to give ordinary authority due respect without giving it ultimate allegiance.

The young man I'll call Andrew crossed my path in the midst
of a soul-defining struggle with his dad. The father, extremely
conservative socially and religiously, was highly controlling and
harshly critical. His deeply spiritual son had begun to explore
Christian practices and beliefs older and broader than his
father's tightly managed faith—albeit still within the conservative evangelical world.

The breach began when Andrew's father started criticizing
the twenty-three-year-old for not being theologically correct
enough. The father, who had been attentively loving toward
Andrew as a young and pliable child, was incapable of brook-
ing any departure from his rigid religious and political beliefs.
His comeback to Andrew's ideas was prosecutorial, full of
denunciations and warnings about the risk of divine judgment
for incorrect belief.

As Andrew was pelted with repeated barrages of Bible verses,
he began to feel "as if I were drowning, a wave rising up to my
neck." Summoning the courage to challenge this barrage was not
easy in the face of his own doubts and fears: What if his father
were right about Christian doctrine? What if he was being led
astray by new ideas? What about "honor your father"? Facing

down these fears, he called his father and "stood up to him in a way I had never done."

Still the barrage did not stop, with yet another accusatory letter from the father. "I realized I had a decision to make," Andrew told me. "My natural inclination was to return fire for fire, but in the process of praying and reading, I glimpsed, as if far off, what it would mean to be truly myself in Christ—to stand without retort or rebuttal, without the need to prove myself to him." He felt called to move out of the battle of egos that had developed. "At that moment," Andrew said, "I saw my dad's responses as his attempt at love, however distorted, and I laughed. That didn't mean I was going to jump right back into the relationship. I needed to strengthen my choice neither to give in nor to fight." He wrote his father a respectful letter asking for a truce and a temporary suspension of communication.

Andrew was following both sides of Jesus' paradoxical summons, so interestingly combined in the Gospel of Thomas version of the teaching: love *and* hate your family as I do. By "hating" his father's intolerant, emotionally abusive behavior Andrew was "loving" the family values of love, respect, honesty, and honor in the face of his father's abuse of power, challenging his father to live into Gospel truths. The son's firm stance chastened the father enough for the attacks to cease. A couple of years later, the father appeared at Andrew's wedding and received Communion with his "heretical" son. All is not healed, but the bonds are not severed, and the father's heart was stretched a bit further open.

Few people reading these words have not faced a struggle in adolescence or adulthood to establish their own identity over and against some aspect of their parents' values—to become their "own person," as we put it. In a metaphor as violent as Jesus' own use of "hatred," we say we must "cut the apron strings" in order to grow up. Breaking with the past has become such second nature, a rebellion that just won't quit, that it may nowadays be a virtue taken to excess. Our countercultural task may be to value tradition more highly! Every age and situation must find its own appropriate balance.[4]

Jesus embodied this balance by avoiding a total break with his family while refusing to give them ultimate authority. One story tells of time spent with mother and brothers after a wedding in Cana of Galilee (John 2:12), another of a visit with his brothers, albeit a contentious one (John 7:2-10). Was this steadfastness in the midst of disagreement and tension one reason the family ended up finally joining the disciple band (Acts 1:14)?

Fidelity in estrangement has great power. The bond between Andrew and his father was not broken by Andrew's boldness. I know parents who, for reasons they cannot fathom, have become anathema to their children. A son who realized he was gay felt rejected by his mother for reasons the mother could not understand. She respected his request that they not see each other but sent a simple card every few months expressing her acceptance and love. Eventually, to her astonished joy, she received an invitation to his covenant ceremony, and a reconciliation began. Her persistent love in the midst of estrangement bore fruit.

Jesus upholds the structure of the family even as he challenges its determinative power over our souls. These relationships, like the social order itself, are meant to be ruled by the question "What does God desire?" as revealed in Torah, Prophets, and Gospels.

Obey civil authorities but always in the light of God's reign.

Render . . . to Caesar the things that are Caesar's, and to God the things that are God's.

—LUKE 20:25, NKJV

Jesus' challenge to family authority extends beyond blood relations to religious and political authorities, the mothers and fathers of society. When early Christians said they were "in the world but not of it," they didn't mean they weren't part of nature or the human family. Cosmos, or world, for them, was this present world order—the current "principalities" and "powers" of society which exercise enormous psychological and spiritual power for both good and ill. (See Eph. 6:12, KJV.)[5]

Government is necessary, even God-given, since anarchy results in brutality and death. Thus we are, as an early Christian writer tells us, to "honor the emperor." But we are also to "fear God." (See 1 Pet. 2:17.) All government is accountable to a just God. Even purportedly Christian governments, like the apartheid regime in South Africa, are to be judged, situation by situation, and age by age, by the values at the heart of the kingdom proclamation: a radical vision of social equity, personal accountability, compassionate community, just judgment, and respect for creation. "Honor both God and Caesar," Jesus says; but as usual, he doesn't give us a rule book on the specifics of good citizenship in various circumstances. That absence accounts in part for the fact that Christians seldom find themselves of one mind about social issues.

Andrew's challenge to his father's world did not stop with theology. Andrew became convinced that Christian values couldn't possibly support the impending war in Iraq and found himself standing in the cold Minnesota winter wind holding a placard, the butt of jeers and curses from opponents. Andrew's father, had he been there, would have held placards supporting the war. Was one right and the other wrong, or does each have hold of conflicting principles difficult to reconcile?

At the very least, fidelity to Jesus' directive requires that we not accept government authority blindly: "my country right or wrong" has no place in Jesus' world, however deep his devotion to his people and nation may have been. The choice of the Greek word *basileia* to describe God's "kingdom" puts the *basileia* of Caesar, the Empire, or any other temporal establishment in second place after God. "We must obey God rather than any human authority," said those who had been taught by Jesus

(Acts 5:29). This resistance to any government that claims the mandate of heaven as pagans did stretches back to Moses and the prophets and has empowered more than one social revolution inspired or supported by Christians through the ages.

Once in power, Christians banned gladiatorial games and infanticide and organized compassion for the socially marginal and the sick. The drive to abolish slavery, the emancipation of women from legal servitude, and the movement for racial equality all involved Christian participation and have roots in the kingdom vision. These latest revolutions have, of course, been ferociously opposed by other Christians.

During the Vietnam War, I found myself in the middle of just such a conflict. Though no pacifist myself, I worked with more than one young man in my community who felt deeply called to be a conscientious objector. I remember vividly the night I accompanied the teen I'll call Tommy to his draft board hearing. The older men Tommy faced were good citizens, many of them churchgoers, most veterans of World War II. Young men unwilling to go to war for democracy and American national interest were abhorrent to them. Tommy not only felt the war was unjust—not a valid legal reason for exemption from the draft—but that he could not, as a Christian, take up arms. Having given his witness, Tommy was asked to leave the room while the draft board grilled me about the authenticity of his stance. Basically they wanted to know what was wrong with him: mental illness? sexual orientation? cowardice? They honestly considered objections to war such as his a sign of moral or psychological weakness. I defended Tommy's integrity, explained my church's support of his right to claim conscientious objector status, and cited the Gospels. They accepted his petition.

When moral and religious disagreements break out, I believe Jesus calls us to serious debate and discussion rather than the denunciations and demonization that so often characterize such differences. Jesus himself was unjustly pegged as a violent revolutionary and a tool of Satan by religious authorities who claimed the unconditional mandate of God. (See John 11:49-50 and Luke 11:15.)

Still, the time often comes when agreement is not possible, and one or both sides feel called to active witness and radical opposition even to the point of civil disobedience. One could cite many heroic figures in history, but one of my favorites is the woman who chained herself to a large tree on Good Friday in protest against the sacrifice of a wilderness preserve to "progress." This woman, "Helen," had led a legal battle for over twenty years to keep an interstate highway from cutting through a protected wildlife preserve. Legal battle lost, the bulldozers were ready to go, except for this short, wiry woman's body in their way.

It takes more than a bit of pluck for a normally law-abiding suburban matron to go against city, state, and courts, but Helen's love for the earth superseded her respect for the law. She was, unfortunately, doomed to lose the battle, but her protest made the front page of the newspaper the day before Easter. I couldn't help but see in her face a reflection of Jesus' own witness to values deeper and more enduring than the expediency of the marketplace, the power of the government, and the tyranny of the automobile.[6]

Helen is part of a growing company of witnesses who provoke us to think harder about the right use of land as we heedlessly "develop" the earth in destructive ways ruled by our immediate cravings for convenience and comfort rather than the good of whole regions and biospheres. She owes allegiance to something and Someone greater than the marketplace or the government. For her, the trees of the forest are more than raw fodder for human purposes. They are creatures of God, vital parts of the well-being of her region, neighbors to be treated with respect.

QUESTIONS FOR REFLECTION AND DISCUSSION

1. Have you ever had to struggle against family pressure to be your best self? How? In what ways has your family background supported your growth toward moral and spiritual maturity?

2. In what ways does Jesus support family values? In what ways does his teaching challenge the power of the family? the government?

3. What is the role of the Christian in the face of governmental injustice? the role of the church? How should Christians seek to implement social compassion and justice in a democratic society? When, if ever, is civil disobedience justifiable?

CHAPTER 6

Practice Simple Justice

"WHAT QUALITIES MAKE for a good neighbor?" Jesus asks. (See Luke 10:36.) By word and deed he challenges everything in us that would keep us from treating every human being we meet as a neighbor—a "near one"—deserving the same decency and respect we wish to receive ourselves from those we meet. He provokes us to stretch the meaning of the ancient command to "love your neighbor as yourself" (Lev. 19:18) beyond "our own kind" to include whoever crosses our path at any time.

Bad neighbors, everyone knows, can be a trial. Like the woman who leaves her giant German shepherd chained in the yard to bark incessantly, disturbing everyone nearby. Or the new neighbor who, just so he can "get a better view," cuts down trees that straddle your joint property line, providing filtered light for your decades-old shade garden. Such behavior, we say, is "simply not decent."

If we go to court over the devastation of tree and garden, we declare the tree cutting "not just." We call on the law for justice because the law represents the formal social embodiment of decency—those actions that make for the *jus*, or right balance, of give and take between people. The Hebrew Bible calls it *tzedakah*, social justice and personal righteousness all rolled up in one word. Jesus sees it as the everyday expression of *agape*, God's love.

Lack of such simple decency, simple justice, simple equity in relationships may begin with neighborhood irritations. But small and often petty-minded power struggles are the mother of all conflicts, from the moment Cain slew his "neighbor" and brother Abel out of religious envy to a contemporary urban gang war sparked by one kid's killing another over a leather coat. On the other hand, acts of ordinary decency can be openings to the power of God's reign in our midst.

Treat others just as you would want to be treated.

Do to others as you would have them do to you.
> —LUKE 6:3

Whoever gives even a cup of cold water to one of these little ones . . . [will not] lose their reward.
> —MATTHEW 10:42

"You shall love your neighbor as yourself."
> —MARK 12:31

Sometimes all the petty power plays of everyday life dissolve in a revelatory surge of our God-given inseparability from one another. Total strangers apply CPR (cardiopulmonary resuscitation) to heart attack victims, perform the Heimlich maneuver on someone choking in a restaurant, or, like midtown New York shopkeepers after the attack on the World Trade Towers, pass out bottled water to the parched, dust-covered survivors trudging uptown. Soldiers fall on hand grenades to save their buddies, and people risk their lives to rescue someone who is drowning.

Catastrophe can bring out the best in people, revealing, at least for the moment, our innate capacity for God-like behavior. Ego borders drop; compassionate fellow feeling arises naturally; generosity reaches out, overriding our more ordinary, less connected, less compassionate state. Another human being, someone like me, is in trouble. This could be me or someone I love if circumstances were different.

Jesus challenges us to make the fellow feeling that surfaces in emergencies the heartbeat of our everyday consciousness. Cultivating the intention to "do to others as you would have them do to you" awakens our latent empathy—our sense of how our actions feel to others.

Jesus is hardly alone among the great spiritual masters in teaching that this golden rule gets at the heart of being a human being, though usually the rule is stated in the negative. The great Rabbi Hillel's "what is hateful to you do not do to your fellow man" (Talmud, Shabbat 3id) is paralleled by Buddhism's "hurt not others in ways you yourself would find hurtful" (Udana-Vagara 5.18) and echoed by Confucianism, Hinduism, and Zoroastrianism.[1]

Even in its negative form this is good advice, as you never know when the harmful consequences of your own bad behavior may come back to hurt you. I once knew an elegant African woman who, in the early days of the civil rights movement, went into a hair salon for a hair styling. This establishment took a dim view of people of color, and the stylist coldly, deliberately, totally butchered her hair. Unfortunately for the owners, the woman's cousin was a highly placed minister of secret police in her home nation. Strings were pulled. While no one was physically harmed in the retaliation, within a year the hair salon went out of business.

Retaliation, however, typically breeds more retaliation. The proprietors of the hair salon probably disliked people of color even more after they were put out of business. So refraining from the hateful isn't a bad place to start treating others decently. Indecency breeds indecency; injustice inspires retaliatory injustice. Human relations would be much improved if more people responded to this minimal, sensible precept.

But Jesus summons us to bless, not just avoid harm. Agape—actively doing good—is to be the center of our practice. Taoism's "regard your neighbor's gain as your gain, and your neighbor's loss as your loss" or Islam's "desire for your brother what you desire for yourself" gives voice to the same spirit that breathes through Jesus' words.[2]

Treat the least among you as you would treat me.

"I was hungry and you gave me food, I was thirsty and you gave me something to drink, I was a stranger and you welcomed me, I was naked and you gave me clothing, I was sick and you took care of me, I was in prison and you visited me." . . . Truly I tell you, just as you did it to one of the least of these who are members of my family, you did it to me.

—MATTHEW 25:35-36

Jesus tells us to expand our sense of neighbor by becoming more aware of how we treat people over whom we have power. People who are ingratiating to their bosses, pleasant to their colleagues, affable to their neighbors, and even loving to their spouse sometimes treat "underlings" with less than respect. "You have no idea what it's like standing here day after day waiting on people who ignore you completely because they're chatting the whole time to someone else on their cell phones," said a local shop clerk to my wife the other day. "People used to say 'thank you' and 'have a good day' at the end of sales. No more. And that's to say nothing of those who, if they talk to you at all, are downright rude."

Such behavior appalls me, yet I remember with some chagrin my own behavior to an Arab shopkeeper in the Old City of Jerusalem some years back. An American tourist in a hurry on my last day in Israel, I had popped into his T-shirt emporium for a quick browse. He greeted me with the usual courteous Arab-shopkeeper palaver: would I like Coca-Cola? lemonade? perhaps Turkish coffee?

I tried to be straightforward with him: in a hurry, browsing, no time. But the offers of hospitality kept coming. Finally I said with consumer firmness, "No, thank you. I don't see what I want. I need to go."

The shopkeeper looked daggers at me. "You tourists! All you have time for is money. I welcome you to my shop. I offer you hospitality. I am not here just to wait on you. Why do you not take time to be decent? to act like a human being?"

This was a genuine cultural misunderstanding. I had tried to "be human" in my own culture's utilitarian terms. The Arab shopkeeper expected to be a host, then a haggler of price, playing a canny but courteous game, as old as mercantile civilization itself, with a fellow human being. I expected a utilitarian, impersonal encounter. My behavior, albeit unintentional, gave less space for human encounter.

Jesus tells us to treat not only shopkeepers but everyone in need as if God had just crossed our path. And everyone we meet is in some sort of need, if only to avoid one more unpleasant or unjust encounter today.

My wife once objected to my leaving small tips for inefficient service in restaurants as unfair to the waitstaff. Having waited tables during her college years, she informed me that restaurant inefficiency usually derives from poor management, not inattentive waitpersons. I was in danger of using my power as the customer to mistreat someone with less power in the situation. Likewise, on occasion I take advantage of certain friends' lack of assertiveness simply to get my own way. I treat them, in this respect at least, as "underlings."

It may seem superficial to begin a discussion of justice with social manners. Manners, I know, can cover injustice and mask malice. As the psalmist observes, "speech smoother than butter" can cloak a "heart set on war" (Ps. 55:21). But at their best, manners serve as the everyday expression of love-as-decency. The "soft answer [that] turns away wrath" (Prov. 15:1), for example, is a habit that can be cultivated consciously, helping shape the heart toward empathetic understanding as well as heading conflict off at the pass.[3]

We have neither time nor soul enough for a deep personal relationship with everyone we meet, especially in large cities. We cannot encounter every person on a "thou" level, but we can treat each one as "you" rather than the impersonal "it" which robs an individual of dignity. We can treat one another with ordinary decency. As Rowan Williams, the archbishop of Canterbury, brilliantly observes, civic life depends on a form of love, a fundamental charity by which we all decide to treat each other with some measure of decency and fairness, an "equalising of honour or status."[4] Such decency, with its codes and customs, its rules and regulations, is also part of the *tzedekah*—the simple justice—that Jesus calls humanity to embrace as the central practice of social life.

Deciding on specific intentions for dealing graciously with those we encounter can shape our behavior significantly.[5] Such a quiet witness invites others to behave in similar ways. My friend Risa gives to beggars on the subway in New York. For her this practice is not only an act of decency but "a subversive activity," a civil protest against what she sees as the real indecency—public policy that whisks the homeless out of sight rather than address the root causes of homelessness.

No longer can New York's homeless be characterized as the terminal winos. Instead, the homeless population includes thousands of mental patients turned out in the cold in governmental tax-cutting programs. Other thousands are the working poor who literally can't afford housing in New York's overpriced market. To make the city safer, more pleasant, and visitor-friendly, city hall works to keep these people out of public places—solutions that sidestep the deeper systemic injustice of turning mentally ill and economically marginal individuals into beggars.

"The guy enters the subway car," Rise tells our spiritual sharing group. "Everybody ducks behind a newspaper, buries themselves in their book, or carefully contemplates the dirt on the floor. He's invisible. He comes to me. I give him a quarter or a dollar or whatever. Whether this particular beggar is for real or not, the problem certainly is. By this time half the people in the car are watching us. That at least keeps what the man symbolizes in one small sector of the public eye." Risa intends not only to help but to be provocative; she hopes the hearts of some of her fellow subway riders are touched or troubled by actually watching the money exchange hands. Sometimes others pull out change to give the invisible man in their midst—that negligible figure Jesus tells us is the Messiah himself coming to us in disguise.

Pay your taxes: support the community.

Render to Caesar the things that are Caesar's, and to God the things that are God's.

—MARK 12:17, NKJV

Pay the Temple tax for you and for me.

—MATTHEW 17:27, AT

I'm aware of such needs not only when I see a beggar on the subway or respond to the *New York Times* annual Christmas drive for the needy but when I wrestle with my tax forms every spring. Like most people I'm a bit ambivalent about taxes. After all, it's my money, isn't it?

"Well, yes," say Jesus and the prophets, "but not entirely." Even tax-paying is meant to be a spiritual exercise. Not only are taxes the price of civilization, as the late Supreme Court Justice Oliver Wendell Holmes once remarked, but they are a part of simple justice, the fundamental social equity, we owe to others. Participating in society requires these membership dues. If life is not first and foremost communal, there is no security for the personal. How taxes are collected and used depends on era, circumstances, and the economic system, but taxes are an inescapable part of the equation. Some taxes help restore the balance between those advantaged by a particular social system and those disadvantaged by it.

Scripture calls the whole community to be responsible for the well-being of everyone. In both Testaments, God cares about the civil order, not only for the sake of believers but for the whole body politic. Steeped in the ancient Hebrew royal theology, which calls the king to "defend the cause of the poor . . . and give deliverance to the needy" (Ps. 72:4), Jesus holds the "shepherds" of society accountable for the welfare of those most likely to be left out or shortchanged in any social setup. He denounces those who would neglect justice for the poor and helpless. We are not only bidden to "give alms" to the poor personally (Matt. 6:2) but to recognize the just role of taxes in the health of the social fabric.

Jesus made his most famous pronouncement on taxes in response to the question about paying taxes to Caesar. His Zen-like saying, as previously noted, stated a principle without giving a precise prescription. Jesus both affirmed the reality and necessity of government and challenged its claim to ultimate loyalty. Protests against unjust taxation, tax waste, and unjust policies supported by taxes are, on occasion, justified by Jesus' words.

A lesser-known tax tale appears in an odd story from Matthew. (See Matthew 17:24-27.) Peter comes to Jesus with the report that the Temple tax is due. Jesus implies that the disciples are children of the heavenly Father, not the religious establishment. They are ultimately "free." Still, Jesus allows, the tax should be paid "so as not to give offense" either to the authorities or to the common good, which is served by the Temple's charity to the poor, among other things. Finally, Jesus instructs Peter to find exactly the right amount for the tax in the mouth of a fish he catches. Peter pays the tax but not using his or Jesus' money.

The story reads like a riddle: did Jesus actually pay the tax or not? Matthew's Gospel, written for Jewish Christians, probably includes the story in order to support continued payment of the Temple tax. Clearly the reason for paying the tax was its critical importance in sustaining society. "Your ultimate allegiance is to God's reign," Jesus seems to say, "so be good citizens unless it betrays the kingdom." We are left to work out the appropriate response in each situation. On the one hand, early Christians prayed for the emperor and paid their taxes, even to a partially unjust regime; on the other, they refused to worship Caesar's allegedly divine "genius," often to the point of death.

As I prepare my returns for the federal, state, and local municipality taxes—just as when Suzanne and I lay out our annual plans for tithing—I am challenged to remember that we are, willy-nilly, part of a larger whole. The check I write pays for police and fire department, public education, the common space of parks and recreation fields, public transportation, and many other conveniences that give everyone, regardless of income, access to a better quality of life. Some taxes also go to support the disabled, those shut out of the economy, and those whose circumstances make them unable to work.

In democracies we are able, thank God, to debate tax policy and usage. Modern societies have changed ancient patterns, which funneled taxes largely into the pockets of the aristocracy. We may debate how high or low taxes should be, quarrel about how they are spent, debate the relative merits of graduated income tax versus flat tax. But followers of Jesus are challenged to see not only the church but the world as "members one of another" (Rom. 12:5). They are asked to support whatever creates a society where everyone has a place at the table—even the invisible members of a society where only the strong and privileged count.

For a society in which a beggar on the subway and a crazy lady huddled in rags on the steps of the city church would no longer be invisible I'd gladly paste a "Please raise my taxes" sticker on my bumper. It's a matter of simple justice.

QUESTIONS FOR REFLECTION AND DISCUSSION

1. What makes a good neighbor? a bad one? How might any seeking to follow Jesus respond constructively to a difficult neighbor?

2. Think of as many examples of ordinary decency as you can. How do such acts allow relationships and society to function more effectively?

3. What are the best ways a disciple of Jesus can help those with less power, status, or access to opportunity? What examples of such practices have you witnessed or participated in? To what extent can taxes be part of this on a systemic, social level?

CHAPTER 7

Welcome the Stranger

A FRIEND TELLS THE tale of the homeless man who wandered into the elegant sit-down dinner she attended in a relative's parish. This old-line suburban church in a first-ring suburb sits near a poor city. The parish draws an upper middle-class congregation from its neighborhood of large, hundred-year-old homes, and even funds outreach ministries to the poor. But this evening dinner was intended for parishioners, with tablecloths, candles, good china, and all the trimmings.

Into the midst of this convivial crowd the homeless man wandered, probably looking for food or money. "What was remarkable," my friend relates, "is that no one looked at him. Most everyone knew he was there, gaping into the room, looking for a response." In effect, he remained invisible, and after the space of a few heartbeats, shuffled out of the room. Upon reflection, some parishioners wondered why "someone" hadn't gotten up to deal with him and confessed their own discomfort. The man's very presence was a provocation to do good in some way, at least to provide him a meal in the kitchen. As the Syro-Phoenician woman said to Jesus, "even the dogs eat the crumbs that fall from their masters' table!" (Matt. 15:27). One can easily imagine Jesus as one of the diners clearing a space to let the man sit down and join the meal rather than remain unseen. Everyone counts for God, even those uncomfortably different from us.

> *Do good to those who are different from you. Don't let social propriety or religious strictures restrict the outreach of love.*

"Which of these three, do you think, was a neighbor to the man who fell into the hands of the robbers?" He said, "The one who showed him mercy." Jesus said to him, "Go and do likewise."

—LUKE 10:36-37

You shall not oppress the alien.
—LEVITICUS 19:33

"Whenever you did one of these things to someone overlooked or ignored, that was me—you did it to me."
—MATTHEW 25:40, THE MESSAGE

Jesus identifies the invisible homeless man as none other than himself. Whoever is needy, hungry, begging, naked, or merely thirsty is nothing less than the Son of Man, hidden in the guise of an ordinary person.[1]

Jesus uses the term *Son of Man* in a cagey and evocative way, just as he does many of his other sayings. On the one hand, *bar adam,* quite literally "son of earth," could simply mean "human being." On the other hand, Jesus could be referring to the "one like a son of man" in Daniel's vision, a heaven-sent figure whose full and complete God-shaped humanity represents God's desires for human nature (Dan. 7:13). In Jesus' day many believed such a divinely charged figure would usher in the kingdom of God. Because these two meanings exist, scholars battle over which he meant.[2]

As you might guess, I'd much prefer to let the ambiguity stand, believing Jesus probably meant both. He is bold enough to offer his way of being in the world as a clear declaration of God's desire for humanity: he is the Son of Man, God's dream of the truly Human One made flesh. On the other hand, his humanity is not separate from ours but rather a mature revelation of the gold at the heart of our common nature. Every single person, no matter how difficult or different, is *bar Adam*, bearer of the divine image.

The same inhospitable disregard shown to the homeless intruder at an elegant dinner can occur over the slightest differences. I endured a painful "alien" experience quite the opposite of being invisible. I was giving a series of early-morning lectures to a small group for four Sundays at a church that served a wealthy, exclusive urban neighborhood. Each week at the service following the lecture I received what I came to call "the look" from more than one person. A flick of the eyes rakes over you from head to foot; "the look" makes you want to look down to see if, by chance, you have dropped a large dollop of jam on your shirt or worse.

The first couple of times I figured I was being oversensitive, but "the look" followed me to coffee hour, where I was otherwise ignored, even by those who said they had appreciated my talks. The warmth and security of meeting and greeting friends occupied people's attention, and I clearly was not part of their tight-knit circle. *Who is this stranger?* the eyes inquired, but not even a courteous greeting followed. Surely any newcomer would find it difficult to break into this congregation. The look is not limited to such wealthy enclaves, of course. It happens when people of any class, caste, or color prefer to cluster defensively with their own kind.

Other congregations respond differently to people who don't fit their mold, making a point of seeking real diversity. Another affluent congregation hosts the homeless for breakfast and holds annual Thanksgiving and Christmas dinners for anyone who isn't ensconced in the bosom of a nearby family. Senior citizens, the homeless, the well-to-do, and just plain folks of many races mingle happily at these festive occasions.

Social proprieties, especially those linked with religious custom, can become barriers to the manifestation of God's love. A veteran pastor, an austere and serious gentleman, once lectured younger clergy about proper behavior in his small southern town. He related a tale about his own ministry in which a weeping wife had begged him to go into the next county to fetch her alcoholic husband from a popular bar. She was terrified he'd kill himself driving home. The pastor, who belonged to a temperance church, preached against drinking, and "had never darkened the door of a bar," went out late at night, drove to the next county, and entered the smoky den of iniquity. There he found the parishioner dead drunk, got him to his feet, and headed out to his own car.

Listening to this somewhat prim man, my heart was warmed. Other clergy were smiling at his loving outreach. What a magnificent story of pastoral care! What a wonderful example of the Good Shepherd seeking the lost sheep! I thought surely he'd end his dramatic story with that parable. No such luck. Much to my dismay, his conclusion careened wildly in another direction. "As I staggered to the car with this drunken man, I saw one of my church leaders drive by in a car. She saw me and gave me such grief the next week I never did anything like that again. I tell you, stay out of those places, no matter what, if you know what's good for your reputation!" More than one clergy face in that audience went from spellbound to stunned, though a few nodded in agreement.

Jesus himself was famous, or infamous, for going into all the wrong places, depending on your angle of vision. The religiously correct disapproved of his hobnobbing with outright sinners. His poor followers probably questioned his meals with the rich. Even his disciples were shocked by his manifest compassion for wayward women.

His most famous story sharply challenges all the ways social and religious propriety and the demands of sacred ceremony can undercut the recognition of common humanity (Luke 10:25-37). The people who leave a comatose robbery victim to die on the dangerous road from Jerusalem to Jericho are

Temple functionaries, a priest and a Levite. Did the priest fear that the victim, if dead, might plunge him into a state of ritual uncleanness, thereby temporarily unfit to come ritually into the presence of God? Was that so important he couldn't at least investigate? Did the Levite put Temple obligations before the act of human caring? Jesus doesn't say, inviting us to ponder the "priest" and "Levite" in our own experience and all the reasons they might avoid getting involved.

Jesus' audience may have applauded his criticism of the widely resented Temple aristocracy, but they can't have been happy about the surprise ending to the story. The half-dead Jewish man's rescuer is none other than one of those neighboring half-breed heretics, a Samaritan, whom Jesus holds up as more faithful to the Torah than the Jewish leaders.

The Samaritan understood or followed instinctively the original meaning of the commandments in the Hebrew tradition, which arose among nomads in the deserts of the Middle East. Hospitality and care for strangers ranked high in moral urgency, extending even to enemies in need of food or drink.[3] Somehow in a world of fierce tribal pride and intertribal warfare, the common humanity of the stranger was recognized and placed at the apex of the moral hierarchy.

For Jesus to celebrate a Samaritan as the example of an Israelite true to the spirit and letter of the Torah must have deeply offended many. Samaritans and Jews were divided by what Freud called "narcissism of small differences." The rivalry goes back almost a thousand years to the split between the northern and southern Israelite kingdoms. In Jesus' day, both groups followed a similar text of the Torah, though with different interpretations, and worshiped the one unseeable God of creation, shunning idolatry. But though both were descendants of ancient Israelite stock, a mixture of Hebrew and Canaanite blood, Samaritans continued the custom of foreign intermarriage rejected by postexilic Judeans. Judeans considered Samaritans religious enemies. Samaritans returned the hostility.

As so often in human history, religious strictures and social differences fueled a fierce xenophobia which Jesus challenges in word and deed. Unlike many of his contemporaries, he does not avoid traveling through Samaria, engaging Samaritans in deep conversation, or even welcoming Samaritan followers. (See Luke 9:51-56; John 4:1-42.)[4] For his trouble, his enemies slur him as a demon-possessed Samaritan (John 8:48), including him in their contempt for the hated group. Similarly, bigots through the ages have demonized any who hang out with "those people," whoever they may be. More alike than different among the nations of the world, Judeans and Samaritans allowed their differences to obscure their common humanity. Like countless groups throughout history, they saw each other through xenophobic eyes.

Welcome and love the stranger.

"I was a stranger, and you welcomed me."
—MATTHEW 25:35

How we react to the stranger—someone alien to us—fundamentally tests our humanity. It's natural for the stranger—and for strange customs, cultures, and ideas—to evoke suspicion. Because the unknown may contain hidden danger, our urge to investigate the stranger is a necessity, not a flaw in our character. We rightly tell our children not to go off with strangers. But fear of the unknown may intensify beyond reason into the blind revulsion and rejection of xenophobia, as it did for ancient Jews and Samaritans.

Feared strangers easily become, in our thinking, less human than we. The picture of the alien remains the same, whatever time or place: the other is less intelligent but more devious, morally inferior, often dirtier, more impulsive, and less attractive.

On the other hand, the very same strangeness may not only pique our interest but blossom into xenophilia—an intrigued, fascinated love of that which is different. Both xenophobia and xenophilia are parts of our survival equipment. Xenophilia inspires fascination with the new and different. It invites us to encounter strangers with an initially positive, inquiring interest rather than knee-jerk suspicion. Intriguing strangers become doorways into new aspects of the human experience, valued expansions of our sense of the world.

The Hebrew scriptures go so far as to command xenophilia: "You shall love the stranger" (Deut. 10:19). The look we're meant to give the stranger is one of interested welcome and exploratory relationship. If we see everyone as fellow citizens of the planet, children of God to be treated with inquiring respect, then fear takes a backseat, serving as appropriate caution while we explore the unknown, but not ruling the situation.

When the friend I'll call Marjorie ran across the stranger on her early morning walk, he appeared lost and unhappy. The African American man, in an almost exclusively white suburb, had run out of gas and was feeling very much an outsider as he stood outside the library. As someone who drove through this elite suburb to and from work, he knew people of color were sometimes stopped and asked their reason for being there. They might be ticketed for what people of color wryly call "driving while black."

The meeting seemed sheer serendipity. On a less graced morning, suspicion might have been Marjorie's reaction. But she had decided, as she started out on the walk, to "let the dog do the leading." Jay-Jay pulled her along the road to the library, a route they didn't usually take. Having decided to go with the flow, she accepted that the stranger she encountered was someone the Spirit had brought her. Did he need help? Her sympathy was immediately kindled. She offered to lend him her own gasoline can, drive him to get gas, and then take him to his car. Would he mind walking back to her home?

The man, clearly stunned by this offer, immediately asked if she wanted identification. He pulled out his wallet, telling her about his background, trying to assure her he was a regular, upstanding citizen. At first perplexed by this response, she soon realized that, of course, she was a lone white woman with a strange man—and a black man at that—on almost-deserted streets. Most of her friends would think she was crazy to invite a stranger of any race back home. She sensed a momentary inner flurry of doubt, checked out her intuitive sense of the situation, and felt safe.

"Meeting him was so much a part of the flow of letting go and letting the dog lead me," she says, "that it just seemed right—as if Jay-Jay had led me right to him." The two strolled back to her garage, got the gasoline can, got gas, drove to the library, and the man went on his way.

Marjorie later received a note of thanks saying that to be befriended, trusted, and helped by a white stranger in such a graceful way had touched some very sore places in this man's soul with healing. He was all too accustomed, in her community, to the look that said only one thing: *What are you doing here?*

When confronted with a stranger, Marjorie could have chosen her apprehensions. But she made a decision for interest rather than suspicion, inquiry rather than avoidance. Her welcome of the stranded motorist not only had provided practical assistance for the man but had lessened his burden of estrangement.

Don't stay behind the walls of your own group.

If you greet only your brothers and sisters, what more are you doing than others? Do not even the Gentiles do the same?

—MATTHEW 5:47

Jesus would have done no less than Marjorie did. His compassionate xenophilia challenged his own world of intense ethnic clannishness and religious cantankerousness, perhaps even elements of prejudice in his own background and makeup.[5] He created in his fellowship a microcosm of the whole society, not just a segment of it. Groups that easily become estranged were all gathered in: rich and poor, strictly religious and slackly observant, the morally upright and those with shady backgrounds, political radicals like Simon the Zealot and establishment folk like the beloved disciple, and, perhaps most astonishingly for his day, women together with men.[6]

Reaching even beyond the borders of his own fellowship, Jesus literally touched the untouchable, like lepers and ritually impure women, with healing power and restored them to community.[7] As the Gospels tell it, he even went into Phoenicia and the Greek Decapolis, or "Ten Cities" confederacy of Galilee, taking his good news of God's welcome to non-Jews (Mark 7:24-37).

Jesus called estranged groups into one spiritual neighborhood and family, teaching each group to look beyond the surface of difference among people to the human essence of a person. It comes, therefore, as no surprise that the first major controversy in the early Christian community was over exactly how to admit non-Jews to full fellowship. Nor is it strange that a converted enemy, Saul of Tarsus, claimed to hear the risen Christ Jesus demanding that these "Gentile" strangers be fully accepted as full disciples of Jesus without undergoing ritual conversion to Judaism. The historical Jesus apparently left no such membership directions, and some disciples resisted Paul vigorously. But the extravagant embrace of the stranger in Jesus' ministry made such an all-embracing welcome virtually inevitable.

In our day we seem to face strangers at every turn, both on TV and on the streets. In my own north New Jersey region, the mostly upper middle-class commuter community where I minister now boasts over thirty languages spoken in the homes of elementary school pupils. This diversity usually enriches and pleases but on occasion leads to clashes between groups. Difference can provoke either hostility or the desire to understand better. Our small suburban city's leadership intentionally encourages cooperation and understanding among people of varying backgrounds. In one effort, citizens of different racial backgrounds come together for Study Circles, in which racial prejudice is confronted head on.[8]

But good intentions alone will not suffice. Politeness carries us only so far. Only the genuine connection of common humanity that Jesus challenges us to see in the other will change the heart.

I was part of a Study Circle leadership training seminar led by a trained facilitator, an African American businessman I'll call Clarence, who had a good position in a major corporation. The leadership group of well-intentioned black and white folks had shared childhood experiences that had shaped their views of race as well as ways we had seen prejudice in action.

The white participants had just been deeply moved by one African American woman's tale of mistreatment in her high school years at the hands of well-meaning whites who unconsciously patronized her. An embarrassed silence had settled in the room. Finally one of the leading white proponents of diversity broke it by saying, "Maybe this is part of the dilemma. We're so polite with one another we don't say what we really feel." I chimed in, adding, "I often feel I'm walking on eggshells with people of other races, because I don't know in advance what might offend. So I'm always a bit edgy."

The facilitator looked me straight in the eye for a long ten seconds before replying. "What makes you think that's any different from the way I feel? I've been walking on eggshells every day of my life as a black man in a white world."

Suddenly the barriers between all of us came down. That moment truly launched the interracial dialogue project because we were all, for a moment, just human beings uneasy and afraid about how to relate to one another. The facilitator smiled and chuckled. I laughed in relief. After that exchange, we all got more real with each other. The *jus* had appeared— the balance at the heart of simple justice. We were all in the same boat as vulnerable human beings rather than socially dominant white facing minority black—all simply *bar adam*, children of earth.

Letting this sense of common humanity soften the edges of our differences is a challenge humanity has faced from its beginnings. The early Christian church prided itself on drawing people from "every tribe and language and people and nation" (Rev. 5:9) but soon fell into its own forms of xenophobia, vilifying heretics, persecuting Jews, and suppressing the native European pagan religion. The man Jesus, a Jew of the first century of our era, was not a modern internationalist, but the implications of his vision and the rich diversity of the community he created during his lifetime have much to say to our century.

The old white Christian nations of Europe are becoming more ethnically and religiously diverse. Canada and Australia absorb new immigrants. The clash of Native Americans and descendants of Spanish and Portuguese invaders continues in Central and South America. In the United States, multiple ethnic, racial, and religious interests challenge the cultural hegemony of white Protestants, even as the old black/white divide continues to produce injustices. More urgently than ever before, the biblical mandate to "show hospitality to strangers" (Heb. 13:2) summons us to create a world where nonuniformity breeds not estrangement but engagement. Every encounter, however small, which forms grace-filled links between diverse groups is part of that effort.

The common problems humanity faces in the twenty-first century call for greater cooperation between nations and religions than ever before. We all participate in the problems, so all of us are needed for the solutions. We're all in this together.

QUESTIONS FOR REFLECTION AND DISCUSSION

1. Have you ever experienced being the "alien" or "odd person out" in a situation? How did people treat you? How would you like to be treated?

2. In what ways can we "welcome the stranger"? Be as specific as possible about real situations.

3. Who are contemporary "Samaritans"—despised or maligned groups—in your community? the nation? the world? What does Jesus' story of the Good Samaritan have to teach us about relating to them?

CHAPTER 8

Trust That the News Is Ultimately Good

JESUS' CALL FOR cooperation with the kingdom's cause is not universally embraced. His provocative words and deeds evoke resistance and rejection as well as new discovery for those who rise to his challenge. His own disciples deserted and betrayed him. Religious and political opponents plotted against him and finally succeeded in killing him.

People choose for or against the gospel proclamation. All over the world people reject other paths of wisdom like Jesus' that lead to life, opting instead for short-term gratification of their lesser selves, a self-destructive choice. Parts of our own soul resist the grace of God which would change them if we accepted the yoke of Jesus' practice. We may all be in this together, but we're not all headed in the direction of solutions that will make the earth flourish and lead humanity toward justice and peace.

What about those who resist the way that leads to life?

Jesus speaks both of severe judgment and of profound mercy for all who resist the complete coming of God's reign. It is crucial to see how these two polarities are balanced. On the one hand, Jesus tells stories full of dire warning. Feckless wedding attendants are shut out of the marriage feast because they are late in fulfilling their duties (Matt. 25:1-13). A rich man wakes up in hell-fire because he neglected a poor man outside his gate (Luke 16:19-31). Many will weep in envy as others feast with Abraham, Isaac, and Jacob at the messianic banquet when the kingdom comes fully.

On the other hand, Jesus tells stories about a love that will never desert us, no matter how far we wander from it. A shepherd who loses just one of his hundred sheep does not give up the search until he finds that sheep and brings it home. A woman loses one precious coin—perhaps out of the dowry necklace she wears—and will not stop searching until she recovers it. A father runs to embrace an errant son the moment he sees him coming. (See Luke 15.)

Are these stories of divine severity and mercy yet another of the paradoxical pairs that characterize Jesus' teaching? Rabbinical circles before and after Jesus' time spent considerable time debating the balance of justice and mercy, divine severity and divine love. Many of these discussions ended in the affirmation that God's judgment always serves loving mercy, not punitive vengeance. God is even pictured praying to himself, "May my mercy always triumph over my wrath."[1]

Because Jesus affirms that the Divine Love will not give up on any lost sheep until it is found, I have come to believe that we must read stories of warning in the light of the stories of mercy, not the other way around. That is certainly the way Paul of Tarsus, the first recorded commentator on the Gospel message, understood it. No slouch on sin and judgment, he concludes his own rabbinical version of Jesus' message in good paradoxical style: "God has imprisoned all in disobedience *so that he may be merciful to all*" (Rom. 11:32, emphasis added). Yes, mercy will have the last word. But don't make trouble for yourselves. Pay strict attention to warnings about the hell-to-pay down certain roads.

For example, the story of the foolish bridesmaids late for the wedding can be read as a strong warning about the danger of missing opportunities to respond to grace, or as Jesus puts it, a warning to "keep awake" rather than a statement of ultimate doom. In certain life situations, unpreparedness makes us miss a God-given opportunity that will never come again. Likewise the story about the rich man in torment is designed, quite deliberately, to frighten rich folk who use their fortune only to indulge themselves into paying attention to the clear teachings of Torah.

When Jesus is asked point-blank, "Will only a few be saved?" he doesn't answer the question directly. Instead he urges the listeners to take seriously their own day-by-day choices that lead into the fullness of life God offers the human race. Beware, he warns, lest you take the path that leads to self-destruction (Luke 13:23-30).

Don't take the path to the garbage dump but the road to life.

Enter through the narrow gate; for the gate is wide and the road is easy that leads to destruction. . . . The gate is narrow and the road is hard that leads to life, and there are few who find it.

—MATTHEW 7:13-14

Many of us modern folk don't like religious figures using the scare tactics Jesus sometimes employs. Our Enlightenment ideal is dispassionate decision making based on calm discussion of competing opinions. We believe religion should inspire us, gently, to be nicer people.

But life itself is a paradoxical combination of generosity and severity. Air is abundant, but if we step off into deep water without knowing how to swim, we won't be able to breathe. Jesus, like the prophets before him, knows that both personal and communal history abound with examples of choices that led to disaster. Because he senses the goodness of life so intensely, Jesus is at great pains to warn us away from all that spoils and destroys. God may be determined that, in the end, all will come to fullness of life, but that doesn't mean we can't make a hell out of our lives right now or that we can't turn any situation hellish for others.

Jesus warns us, in no uncertain terms, to avoid such hells. To describe the anguishes we can create, Jesus uses the widespread rabbinical image of his day: *Gehenna*, that is, the Valley of Hinnom outside the western walls of Jerusalem, the city garbage dump where the fire that burns the refuse "is never quenched" and the worm that eats spoiled food "never dies" (Mark 9:47-48). Hell is the pit of bitterness, the tortured state where we lie tormented by the fire of our own resentment and rage or eaten up by our own despair. Better to cut off your right hand than fall into that state! (See Matt. 5:30.)

Most of us have seen or been people who slowly wander down this broad road, investing in grievance, nursing injury, creating hostility, choosing isolation, or fearfully hoarding in greed until it's hard to reverse course. When deeply injured, I've certainly felt the pull of this dark call in myself.

Don't go there, Jesus warns severely. Take the narrow path that leads to life instead, he advises. The path to fullness of life is aptly described as "narrow" not because God is narrow-minded but because life itself is exacting. Addicts know this well. As they begin recovery, they face the difficult challenge to the illusory "freedom" of following their personal cravings. Only one choice is possible: no alcohol or drugs; and only this "narrow" choice makes health possible.

I once watched helplessly as a young man wandered deeper and deeper into a garbage dumb of addiction, was "found," and then began to crawl his way out. "Cary" was one of the brightest kids in a church youth group—emotionally sensitive, intellectually inquiring. Underneath his interested demeanor, though, dark emotional currents lurked. His father was cold and unfeeling; his mother, sweet but rather helpless. Cary's sense of self was fragile when he graduated from high school and ventured into Manhattan to pursue acting. I lost touch with him for many years and wondered what had become of him.

One day, out of the blue, Cary phoned, wanting to be back in touch. He said he'd been to hell and had a lot he wanted to share. By a coincidence that seemed providential I was due to visit his southern city. We met for dinner. Afterward, on a walk through the park in the gathering twilight, a painful tale poured out: descent into an addiction-fueled madness that culminated with petty theft and begging on the streets. After almost a decade in and out of a drugged half-life, someone succeeded in taking him to an AA meeting. The accepting friendships he made there finally enabled him to make the difficult choice to turn to his Higher Power. Cary found it hard to believe in God because he couldn't understand how God could let all the evil in the world happen, but his Higher Power was helping him stay off drugs. He wanted to know if this Higher Power was what God was really like.

"The God I know," I told Cary, "is a love that can work with you to bring good out of the worst kinds of difficulties. Looks like that's what the Higher Power is doing for you, doesn't it?" He agreed but wondered how to explore this Power more deeply. He found so much about the idea of God confusing.

"Don't worry about understanding how God and the universe run just yet," I cautioned. "Just do what you're doing. Turn to your Higher Power and ask for help as you take the next step. AA says it well enough: one day at a time. Trust your Higher Power to help you live your new life."

Cary can't use alcohol or drugs. No exceptions. The same might be said for choosing forgiveness over revenge or courage over cowardice. Reactive anger often seems easier than considered restraint; fleeing easier than facing difficulty. Not only individuals but whole societies are lured by dark impulses, base cravings, or mere desire for convenience to choose easy paths to destruction. The consequences can be severe.

Miraculously the narrow choice begins to free the self more and more to choose the good previously spoiled by addiction or emotional poison. We find the road to fullness of life narrow only at the beginning and wide with increasing possibilities as we walk it.

More than any prophet before him, Jesus seems to promise that even if we rush willingly into disaster, the Divine Love will not stop until we are made right. When the Jesus of the Gospels finds people in hell, like the insane man possessed by the "legion" of demons which have forced him to wander in lonely places and beat himself with rocks, Jesus wraps the power of God's love around them, enters deeply into their suffering, and brings them out (Mark 5:1-20). Early Christians believed Jesus had entered into hell in just this way to free those once disobedient in the Flood and, indeed, Adam and Eve, symbolizing the whole of humankind. The dire consequences of self-destruction had led the sinners to hell. Divine Love eventually lured them out.[2]

Indeed, Jesus speaks of a "regeneration" of the world, and the the apostles speak of an *apocatastasis*, or "standing up" of all things. (See Matt. 19:28 and Acts 3:21.) God will not stop until all is made right for everyone: "It is not the will of your Father in heaven that one of these little ones should be lost" (Matt. 18:14). Other sections of the New Testament seem to support this view. Paul, who says mercy will triumph over judgment, also declares that "as all die in Adam, so all will be made alive in Christ" (1 Cor. 15:22). And the letter attributed to Peter teaches that souls can be released from the "prison" created by their folly even after death (1 Pet. 3:19-22; 4:6). Even if Cary had died in his addicted hell, totally in doubt about God, the Divine Love would not cease seeking to turn him toward the light. Along with many Christians through the ages, I believe the news Jesus brings is ultimately good for all humanity.[3]

I bring you good news. Trust it.

Believe in the good news.
—Mark 1:15

Many interpreters of Jesus' message resolve this issue differently. Judgment rules; severity triumphs over mercy; condemnation prevails over persistent love. The "good news" becomes "bad news" for all but the chosen few, a veritable "doomspell."

This doomspell has always been a popular version of Jesus' teaching, perhaps for the same reason so many people love disaster movies and horror flicks. If you fantasize about the worst that can happen, maybe you can rehearse ways to escape the catastrophe. Or there's the self-esteem bonus of being among the special few—the very few—who make it. This line of reasoning provides a powerful and subtle temptation to worship and placate God as Threat.

My wife and I heard this doomspell set forth vividly on a visit to the church of my childhood one Sunday morning. This group of otherwise decent, salt-of-the-earth folk practiced a particularly exclusionary kind of rule-bound religion, full of ultimate threats. In the church foyer they were warm, generous, smiling. Entering the precincts of worship, a resigned grimness settled over their sobered faces.

I was praying to understand better the negative face of this kind of religion, and it soon revealed itself clearly. The evangelist's sermon, as customary in this church, pivoted on the question *How can you secure your eternal salvation?* Pastor "Rick," a sweet guy I'd known during my adolescence, began his sermon with a blood-chilling passage from 1 Kings 13 about an obscure prophet who disobeys a minor detail of God's instructions to him and is killed by a lion in spite of faithful obedience in every other way. This ancient tale was read as a paradigm of God's way with us: "This tells us, doesn't it," Rick intoned, "what will happen to all who do not obey the gospel?" The sermon proceeded to outline this church's path to salvation, which is highly legalistic. I've heard similar renditions of this message in less legalistic churches, basically deducing that if you miss the one right way to be saved, too bad for you.

My wife, raised in a more generous spiritual sensibility, gripped my arm till it hurt. "This is monstrous," she whispered. "Just so," I whispered back. "I've just now realized we were all unknowingly brought up to think of God as a monster." How else would one honestly describe such a harsh parent, mayor, or head of government?

I could see all the more clearly why it had taken me so long to live into a trusting relationship with God and why I had to "die" to that old image of God before trust could deepen. When I lived under the power of such a monster-god, I tended to detach myself from God, to go into hiding when I was in the grip of sin or some aspect of self I considered unacceptable: bad-temperedness or bitter anger, prurient interest or lust, or the dark pleasures of unkindness. These were aspects of self "disobedient to the gospel" when understood as rules to be lived up to. These parts of myself were to be shunned in shame, perhaps whispered in confession, left outside the realm of grace. Such piety promotes a pattern of going AWOL from God in order for immature parts of the self to let off steam, then repenting over broken rules, then asking forgiveness for being a bad kid.

The divine grace Jesus proclaims is more transformative than that pattern. Salvation is not first and foremost about the afterlife but about gradually growing into God's image and likeness, so that we can participate in the movement of God's grace through the world. In theological language, being "called, justified, sanctified, and glorified" constitutes one life-changing process. By responding to Jesus' challenges and asking God's help as our response unmasks both strengths and weaknesses, we begin to "co-work" with God (2 Cor. 6:1).

Progressively we are freed from our lesser, fear-driven selves and are able to grow up into the strength of our best, God-given potentials—the "better angels of our nature," to borrow Abraham Lincoln's felicitous phrase. Gradually the soul-crippling power of arrogance, anger, lust for control, resentment, and revenge is broken. We are freed to learn more skillful ways of loving and doing what is good, thus entering more deeply into God's domain on earth.

In order for this grace to work with the whole of our being,

we must share every part of ourselves with God, not just the cooperative parts. Every personality, an amalgam of many different
inner selves, is a rough committee meeting that does not always
come to consensus, divided as it is among conflicting desires and
beliefs. We do not even know our own minds. We are quite often
of more than one mind about most anything from the trivial to
the serious.

Part of the good news is that Christ welcomes every member
of our inner family, noble and ignoble alike, into the presence
of an accepting and challenging love, just as he welcomed all
sorts and conditions of people to his table. He invites us to learn
love for our whole self by letting God love every part of us.

"Declare it all" was the advice of the desert fathers, those radical early Christians who took with great seriousness Jesus' challenge to transform the heart. Declare it all—every thought, every
feeling, every cruel intention, every ignoble desire and holy aspi-
ration. Don't be afraid to present anything to God as it comes into
awareness, because you are beheld by a comprehending, compassionate love that knows how to heal your distempers. Everything
becomes grist for the mill in spiritual growth, even the hells into
which we wander. Some elements will be strengthened, some
diminished, but grace can work with it all.

We are converted one aspect of the self at a time. That phenomenon explains why some parts of us can be approaching
holiness while others remain locked in resistance and rebellion.
Because different parts of our soul proceed at different rates, the
invitation to love with our "whole heart" is the work of a lifetime and beyond. The struggle to bring all the conflicting parts
of our psyche into the conversation takes lots of time, loving
attention, forgiveness, and self-acceptance. But with patience, we
can often find a good hidden in the most difficult and ornery
aspects of the self.

Jesus' message offers good news for the whole self as well as
the whole human race. Living in the presence of a God "to whom
all hearts are open, all desires known" means God scrutinizes

our immaturities with the eye of love, not the glare of condemnation. Such love, merciful even in its judgments, accepting even in its challenges to our behavior, trains us in how to see the whole world.

Be willing to see the potential good in anyone.

Be merciful, just as your Father is merciful.
—LUKE 6:36

[God] makes [the] sun rise on the evil and on the good, and sends rain on the righteous and on the unrighteous.
—MATTHEW 5:4

Everyone counts for God, not just the currently righteous. Jesus saw beyond the ordinary distinctions that we make when we divide into hostile, opposing groups and encouraged his disciples to do the same.

Earlier prophets had made a ruthless distinction between the righteous and the wicked. The Psalms clearly direct the righteous to shun sinners absolutely: don't talk to them, don't walk with them, don't sit with them, hate even to be in their company. (See Pss. 1:1; 26:5.) Other Psalms revel in what can only be called a "holy hatred" for the wicked: "Do I not hate those who hate you, O Lord? . . . I hate them with perfect hatred" (Ps. 139:21-22).

Jesus went against this tradition by welcoming people of all manner of moral richness or deficiency into his presence and breaking bread with them. Rich and poor, observant and nonobservant, truly good and truly deviant: Jesus was not afraid to meet any of these, even if he ended up giving them a strong prescription for better living.

Jesus challenges his disciples to grow up into a love as compassionate as God's: "be merciful, just as your Father is merciful," shedding love on good and wicked alike (Luke 6:36). Such compassion doesn't mean we let hateful people burn crosses on other people's lawns, vicious people get away with attacks, or robbers roam the streets at will. We must make strategic assessments about the moral quality of other people's behavior.

Jesus is not so foolish as to toss moral assessment of right and wrong, good and evil, out the window in the name of some intoxicating acceptance of everything anyone does because "God loves them." Still, his willingness not to shut people out on the basis of negative character aspects calls us to look more deeply for the good possibilities in others, however difficult or dangerous they may appear.

In commonplace ways I keep learning this truth again and again. A member of a nonprofit board I once chaired, "Herb," repeatedly hijacked the conversation with his obsessive anxiety about the possible downside of any proposal. Others would argue with him, fueling his fears. Conversational brawls would bog down the meeting, forcing me into assertive interventions. We had to adopt rules for conversation that still barely contained Herb's skill at negative assessment. I regretted we'd ever nominated him to the board.

This regret persisted until the day Herb sat quietly through a long and increasingly confusing planning discussion, then finally offered his objection at a pivotal moment. With uncanny accuracy, Herb nailed an issue none of us was noticing. Somehow, his comment dispelled our befuddled fog. New ideas emerged, and in short order our plans were headed clearly and constructively in a new direction. After that, I began to listen behind Herb's anxious ditherings for his deeper concern, which often had merit. We learned how to use Herb's fears constructively, even when we voted against his suggestions.

Of course, Herb wasn't really among the wicked, just the annoying. But you never know when someone you consider worse than useless or who stands on the other side of a conflict will turn out to be part of the solution. Persecutors of Jesus' message like Paul of Tarsus become apostles; former terrorists like Menachem Begin lead peace efforts; and violent street gangs turn into constructive community groups. Jesus' radical ability to see how the difficult—even the dangerous— belong to the whole picture from God's viewpoint grows out of Hebrew tradition. Strands of Hebrew thought rise above the absolute black-and-white, good-and-evil stereotypes of many familiar passages. The Wisdom writers and the prophets stress God's universalism as well as Israel's chosenness. They also present the ability of Divine Wisdom to accomplish good ends for Israel and the whole world even through Israel's enemies.[4] In the end, this prophetic strand says, Israel's worst enemies will be reconciled and the world will blossom with peace.

Because God intends our enemies to be our allies and friends someday, Jesus insists that we pray for them. Such universalism is a challenge to any age. People find it far easier to write off individuals, even whole groups, as evil than to maintain a sense that we're all in this together and need to work out differences. But today's enemies are tomorrow's allies, as the experience of America with Germany and Japan after World War II demonstrates. Even in the midst of war, we can remember our opponent's humanity and prepare for the day when we will work together again.

Resist it though we may, partnership for a world where compassion and justice rule is God's design for the whole human race.

QUESTIONS FOR REFLECTION AND DISCUSSION

1. Jesus warns us of the danger of our lives ending up in the "garbage dump." In what ways do you think his warning about hell may be true about our lives here and now? hereafter?

2. In what ways do people "resist the way that leads to life"? Are any such resistances alive in your life?

3. "We are converted one aspect of the self at a time." In what ways are you, step-by-step, finding yourself converted to the Way of Christ?

CHAPTER 9

Be Partners in My Work

JESUS BELIEVED HE had a distinctive relationship with the Source of love he called, in the most intimate terms, Abba. This "Father," known in moments of deep prayer, was not an Omnipotence reserving all power to itself but a Generosity desiring to share its energy with everyone willing to join the work of repairing, redeeming, and continuing to build the world.

Rather than basking in a sense of mystical privilege, Jesus was eager to share that relationship with everyone willing to enter his course of training, in which he taught how to "provoke one another to love and good deeds" of the kind that flow from a deep connection with the Divine. (See Heb. 10:24.) "My Father" became "our Father" in a heartbeat when the disciples, probably yearning to feel in their own experience what showed on Jesus' face when he prayed, said, "Lord, teach us to pray" (Luke 11:1).

The disciples had, of course, been praying all their lives as Jews—at mealtimes, on the sabbath, at festivals, and in times of need. What they meant was, "Give us a share in the Spirit that catches you up into its bounty when you pray." Jesus was glad to initiate them into his way of praying because his aim with these apprentices was to reveal to them the Spirit's way of working through human nature. The prayer he taught makes them—and us—partners in his work, co-mediators of the "powers of the age to come" (Heb. 6:5) present even now in our midst. The Lord's Prayer joins our hearts to God's kingdom purposes for this world: that through human alignment with the Divine Love, bread will be provided for all; mercy and forgiveness will triumph over hard-heartedness; and evil will not shake us out of our dedication to the good God wills for us.

Join me in my work.

The one who believes in me will also do the works that I do and, in fact, will do greater works than these.
—JOHN 14:12

I caught a small glimpse of these powers of God's reign at work on a trip I took to Rome many years ago as a student. A woman I'll call Trudy was a real annoyance to everyone in the tour group. Highly anxious and painfully needy, her expressions of fear, clinging ways, and inappropriate remarks were a constant irritant and could have made her the group pariah. Instead, this group of well-bred Christian folk responded to her with *agape* in the form of simple courtesy. By some sort of unspoken, perhaps unconscious, collusion, a different person each day "took her on" with patience and charity.

As the days progressed, the rough edges of her anxiety smoothed out; her deep insecurity was calmed; her clinging lessened; and her visage literally changed. Probably for the first time in years she felt accepted, seen, valued. As she trusted this unexpectedly safe environment, the pinched lines of worry disappeared, and it became clear that she was, actually, quite beautiful. A sense of humor emerged, and Trudy began having a really good time. For a blessed fortnight, something of the self imprisoned by Trudy's usual anxieties breathed the air of a larger world, and she grew into a valued and cooperative member of the group, available to delight in the good rather than fearing the unexpected. Though the group had begun by "managing" her, Trudy actually became more lovable.

Whether they knew it or not, these kindly folk were God's partners in bringing good news and healing to Trudy. Joining the outreach of God's love in the world typically starts with "cups of cold water" instead of grand, heroic gestures. One of Jesus' first invitations to his disciples to join his work, as related in John's Gospel, is a request to serve dinner to a large crowd of people. Granted, the story goes on to describe a miracle in which five barley loaves and two fish are multiplied to feed a multitude. The "partnership" of the disciples amounts to nothing more heroic than table waiting. (See John 6:1-14.)

Most people, including practicing Christians, would probably be intimidated if asked, "How have you served God's purposes lately?" because they immediately think of something "important" like missionary work, helping the downtrodden, or joining a protest against injustice. I'm convinced many, if not most, of us cross paths with one or more of God's purposes each day, though we may not realize it. If God is building a new world, not just a church, a great deal of the Spirit's activity is not explicitly religious.

As I lead workshops in a spiritual program called Partners with God,[1] I especially appreciate an exercise called "What Does God Care About?" Participants identify a dozen or more things God cares about according to biblical tradition. Common responses include forgiveness, treating others as you would be treated, helping those in need, healing the sick, and making peace, just to mention a few. Participants then recall an incident in their lives when they played a role in one of these spheres, however small. Much to everyone's surprise, stories abound, once people are looking for the ordinary rather than the heroic. A mother was able to forgive her daughter, just last week. A man made peace between two warring groups at his job. A college teacher brought norms for civility into a mud-slinging debate about sexual orientation in his ethics class, urging students to "speak to others as you would like to be spoken to." You no doubt have stories of your own.

God can use any and all of these ordinary, everyday actions, indeed anything that serves good in the world, as part of God's reign coming into our midst, as well as acts of more heroic stature. When we find ourselves saying, "I wish I had more time to serve God," we need to take a closer look at how we can serve God's purposes in the activities and encounters that fill our days. Those who accept Jesus' invitation to become apprentices are meant to learn how to "walk in the Spirit," as Paul puts it, at all times and in all places. This is not a job; it is a way of living.

Heal the sick; raise the dead.

Proclaim the good news . . . cure the sick, raise the dead, cleanse the lepers, cast out demons.
—Matthew 10:7-8

"Eleanor" worked as an aide in a nursing home when she was in college. A female stroke victim arrived, unable to move or speak, and spent her days staring at the ceiling. What intrigued Eleanor was the "alert and frightened look in her eyes. I knew she was there somehow." Whereas the more harried and experienced staff treated the woman almost as if she were in a coma, "whenever I had some free time," Eleanor told me, "I would sit with her, speak to her, and hold her hand."

One day, when she had several bells ringing for her, Eleanor told the woman she had to go and started to let go of her hand. "She grabbed my hand tightly and spoke for the first time, 'Don't go!'" From this first sign of recovery, the ailing woman slowly grew more animated and eventually returned home. Eleanor was just doing her job, living part of her daily life. But the *way* she was doing it brought new life to a woman others might have given up on. Eleanor partnered with God, participating in Jesus' ongoing healing mission.

Jesus trained others in his way of loving, then in the more specialized skills of preaching, healing, and welcoming sinners with mercy, then sent them out to "proclaim the good news, cure the sick, raise the dead, cleanse the lepers, cast out demons." When he realized his ministry might end in death, he told the disciples the same Spirit that gave him life would be their companion, making his own life alive in their lives.

As a true master, Jesus even wanted his disciples to surpass him: "The works that I do, you will do; and even greater works than these" (AP; see John 14:12). The early Christian writings report that the disciples continued preaching, healing, welcoming, community building, and witnessing against injustice.

I don't think Jesus necessarily meant the disciples would have more power to do extraordinary acts, like raising the dead, than he had. Rather the miraculous power of God's love would spread through the world like yeast through bread dough, inspiring many deeds that partake of the Spirit of Jesus. As John describes, Jesus sees himself as a solitary grain of wheat which, falling into the ground and dying, "bears much fruit" in the form of many grains (John 12:24).

Still, sometimes extraordinary things happen, some of which we're beginning to take so for granted we don't realize how astonishing they are. "When you see life come back under your hands once, you're hooked," a fellow member of the local first-aid squad told my friend Kay after she had witnessed her first CPR resurrection. For Kay, working on the squad is simultaneously job, community service, and part of her discipleship.

On one remarkable day, her crew found the man who had called for help down on his kitchen floor—cold, not breathing. "Someone muttered, 'O God!' and we got down on our knees and began to breathe for him, compressing and releasing his heart so that it would empty and fill and keep his brain alive," Kay related. After an endless ten minutes, the man coughed, tried to sit up, and asked, "What happened?" The crew was so astonished no one could speak, "because we had, inwardly, given up hope. After we'd delivered him to the hospital, we just couldn't leave one another. We needed to be together to absorb the stunning surprise of his survival."

Cardiopulmonary resuscitation (CPR) may be a modern medical technique, but the experience of those first-aid workers is not so far from that of Jesus and the prophet Elisha, both of whom likewise raised the dead—most probably people in a coma who would have died without the intervention of a powerful life force.[2]

My confidence in the stories of Jesus raising people up with just a word increased during my own experience in a particular pastoral case. A doctor phoned and begged me to visit a parishioner hovering near death for the eleventh week in the intensive care unit of our local hospital. Myrtle, whose postrestoration difficulties I've related in another book,[3] had "accidentally" run her car into a telephone pole after the untimely death of her only son. "I can't figure out why she's not getting any better," the doctor confessed. "All her other physical indicators tell me she should be out of the coma, but she isn't. Maybe religion can help."

So I went and in a state of prayer stood beside her bed and talked straight through her coma to her heart. "Myrtle," I said, "I think I know where you are and why you're there." The words just seemed to flow through me. "I'm afraid you just want to die because of your son's death. But there are people here who need you and love you, especially your husband. You've got a choice to make. You can either come back or not. Please, for God's sake, come back."

Young and inexperienced in these matters, I left feeling vaguely foolish, hoping none of the nurses had heard me. In a few hours Myrtle came out of her coma, to great rejoicing among the medical staff. When I visited her, she looked penetratingly at me and said, "You know where I was, don't you? I was with my son, and I didn't want to come back!" She shook her head, as if to discard a bad dream or perhaps a fond wish. "But you came to me and told me to come back; and, well, here I am." She laughed.

Since then I've learned a great deal more about people in comas and seen other wonders, medical and otherwise. Not everyone in a coma is able to come out of it as Myrtle did. Some are so damaged it would be better if they didn't. But I can't help but believe that the Spirit that was in Jesus was with us as I stood at Myrtle's bedside, drawing us both into a continuation of the Master's healing work.

Healing stories of both medical and spiritual healing abound.[4] The mission and message of Jesus, joining other cultural forces like the emerging wisdom of ancient medicine, helped change the world's stance toward sickness. Rather than fate or the punishment of the gods, sickness became an adversary to be fought.

Face the powers of oppression as I do.

Whoever does not carry the cross and follow me cannot be my disciple.

—LUKE 14:27

Sickness and healing, like homelessness and safe shelter, are not only personal issues but social ones as well. Jesus didn't just challenge the personal "demons" of his day that caused sickness and poverty but confronted the systemic "powers that be." The authorities did not crucify Jesus because he blessed babies or told people to be kind to their neighbors. They killed him because they perceived he was fomenting revolution. They were wrong only about the *nature* of his rebellion from the status quo, mistakenly fearing violence.

Jesus made little attempt to hide the revolutionary nature of his challenge to the era's power system. Most provocatively, he seems to have adopted a militant slogan from the Zealots, the resistance group prepared to use violence. The group used the saying "take up your cross" to express being prepared to die at the hands of the Romans for your actions. Hardly the slogan of a man who wants to play it safe.[5] And yet, Jesus' method of resistance and protest is nonviolent: "all who take the sword will perish by the sword" (Matt. 26:52).

In the original setting, "take up your cross" primarily meant to witness against oppression, even at the risk of one's life. I know a man who reported his own company to the government for violating pollution laws after executives told him repeatedly to keep quiet and just do his job. Tragically, the whistle-blower went to jail briefly for the company's lawbreaking. The unscrupulous executives turned state's evidence and let the man take the rap for actions in which he participated unwittingly by virtue of his position before discovering they were illegal and contacting the government. He took this injustice nobly, knowing his witness had not been a mistake, willing to "bear the cross."[6]

Anna, the woman who helped found the temporary residence for the homeless in her county seat, had to put up with disbelief and scorn from some friends in her community who regarded homelessness as the lot of social losers, people who could better themselves if only they tried. People like me who live in safe towns and take the train into the nearby city center can easily develop pictures of people and the world that bear little resemblance to life on the ground.

One night at a dinner party, a neighbor of Anna's said, "I think you're wasting your time with these people. I just don't believe there are any real homeless. They're all just mooching." The dinner party paused as Anna, at the risk of her reputation, informed her heckler with seething calmness that he didn't have any idea what he was talking about. If he cared about the truth at all, he could come to the residence and find out for himself. He did, and he discovered how people at the other end of the social reality live. By so doing, the man was given a chance to see the face of Christ in the poor rather than staring self-righteously at his own prejudices.

Incident by incident, person by person, Jesus' way of facing injustice continues to inspire people to stand up and risk opposition in its service. "Greater works" have abounded: ending the cruel gladiatorial games, stopping infanticide, abolishing slavery, demanding equal rights for women and other minorities, and facing tyranny nonviolently. Christians and other people of goodwill have walked the road Jesus taught and embodied to cultivate a world with more room for justice and more space for loving-kindness, often against formidable hostility.[7]

Trust me. Trust the road I lead you on.

Believe in God, believe also in me.
—JOHN 14:1

I am the way, and the truth, and the life.
—JOHN 14:6

When Jesus challenges his apprentices to trust him, he's asking them to trust the Way he shows them. He's so identified with that Way he says that he *is* that Way. His very name, the "Name by which we must be saved," points not to himself but to the Divine itself. "Jesus" is a translation of *Yeshua* or *Yahoshua*, which means "God is salvation."

Jesus declares himself God's decisive messenger for humanity but does not claim that all God's wisdom is bottled up in him. Rather he serves as a "door" to the divine Wisdom that has woven creation's fabric and taught humanity from its earliest days.[8] "What you see in me," he says, "my trust in God, my deeds of loving-kindness and justice, my persistent yearning for the triumph of God's grace on earth—that is the way of Wisdom." This Wisdom itself is the only way to "obtain friendship with God"—the close communion that makes cooperation possible. (See Wisdom 7:14.)[9]

Like the tennis coach who says, "Watch how I serve the ball" or the dancing instructor who says, "Move as I do and feel in yourself what it feels like," Jesus points beyond himself to the art he teaches. I've learned to teach by having good teachers, to preach by listening to good preachers, to write by reading good writers, to love by being loved. What may begin as mimicking—the elegant word is *emulation*—can, if one is trying to catch the spirit of the art rather than just become a carbon copy of the teacher, second nature.

Gandhi, a man who profoundly loved God but who was not a Christian, caught the Spirit that moved in the man Jesus when he read the Gospels. In Gandhi's mind, Jesus' nonviolent approach to social change linked with his own Hindu belief in *ahimsa*, the way of noninjury, to produce the most successful nonviolent revolution in history—a "greater work" if there ever was one! Gandhi trusted Jesus' Way.

Jesus' invitation to trust the Way can easily get hijacked by doctrinal quarrels. Such debates imply the most important issue related to Jesus is subscribing to various beliefs about him. The Greek word *pistis*, which indicates deep personal trust, has been distorted to mean intellectual belief *about* rather than personal trust *in* Jesus' spirit, sayings, and way of walking in the world. Creedal assertions take precedence over way of life. All who cannot subscribe to the creed are excluded from discipleship.

There's an interesting saying and story about this issue in the Gospels. "Whoever is not against us is for us," Jesus tells the disciples when they want to stop a wandering exorcist from using Jesus' name in his healings because "he is not following *us*" (emphasis added; see Mark 9:38-40). Jesus' bottom line doesn't have to do with membership in a particular group or the precise details of doctrinal belief but with whether we join God's world-creating, world-redeeming work: "the one who does the will of my Father in heaven" enters into the flow of God's Spirit through the world (Matt. 7:21).

It should not be surprising to find signs of this Wisdom in the other religious literature of the world: in Buddha's teaching on compassion, the Hindu sages' doctrine of *ahimsa*, or peaceableness, Lao-Tzu's celebration of reverence and humility, and Mohammed's sense of social justice. According to this view, the Way Jesus walks and decisively embodies—of compassion, love, justice, mercy, forgiveness, and peacemaking—is not confined to practitioners of Christianity. Many other traditions witness to that One Way. Wherever people find and follow these virtues, we see the "marks" of Christ.

Jesus himself invites people to put his words into action if they want to test the truth of his teachings. (See John 7:17.) The original disciples' faith in the truth of Jesus' teaching developed gradually. For some of them it began with inquiry, proceeded to obedience, deepened through training and testing, and culminated in visions of the risen Lord.

"But if people don't believe Jesus is God," more than one person has said to me, "why should they bother to listen to what he says?" Well, I'm tempted to say, my grandmother wasn't God, but I still listened to her wisdom and put a lot of it into practice. Of course, the higher our opinion of Jesus, the more likely we are to take him seriously, so acceptance of his prophetic authenticity or true representation of God-in-human-terms can deepen our desire to follow closely. These beliefs, however, grow solid and strong more often in the act of following his words rather than by some self-enforced "leap of faith."

Of course, if one decides to take Jesus with complete seriousness, leaps of faith in the more ordinary sense will actually be required. This is most acutely true regarding his vision of the kingdom's eventual triumph "on earth as in heaven." His robust faith in God's ability to bring the human venture on earth to full flower is a challenge to believe that everything he stands for will, in the end, prevail against all the ignorance and evil in the world. Building on the dreams of prophets before him, Jesus affirms that, with God's help, righteousness and mercy, peace and justice, will have the last word in human history. His invitation to this radical hope may be his most provocative challenge.

QUESTIONS FOR REFLECTION AND DISCUSSION

1. What do you believe God cares about in the world? What do you feel God seeks to accomplish through human beings? In what ways, however small, have your actions aligned with these divine desires?

2. What does the call to "take up your cross" mean to you? Have you or people you have known resisted oppression—in family, job, community, nation—for reasons of faith? How?

3. Trusting Jesus is described as more a matter of spiritual practice than creedal assent. How does what we believe about Jesus affect our attitude toward his challenges?

CHAPTER 10

Do Not Lose Heart

Then Jesus told them a parable about their need to pray always and not to lose heart. . . . And the Lord said, ". . . will not God grant justice to his chosen ones who cry to him day and night? Will he delay long in helping them? I tell you, he will quickly grant justice to them. And yet, when the Son of Man comes, will he find faith on earth?"—Luke 18:1, 6-8

JESUS LIVED AND BREATHED a passionate commitment to the triumph of God's realm of justice and grace. He faced death rather than give up that vision. His living and dying are votes of confident hope in God's willingness to work with and through human beings until that kingdom is vividly realized among us. Granted the horrifying ups and downs of history and the slow, uphill battle for the kind of wisdom Jesus represents to win the hearts of humanity, having such hope may be the greatest challenge Jesus gives us. Claiming such hope, though, is crucial in our era, when humanity faces some of the greatest provocations to destructive evil—and to creative goodness—we have ever known.

I struggled for a long time to find a glimmer of hope in a world increasingly scary. While I walked the dog, worrying about the impending environmental debacle we face, the threat of nuclear holocaust peaked, faded, then returned again in the new form of nuclear proliferation. The trees, compromised by acid rain and auto exhaust, seemed to call, "When will you hear our cry?" Conventional wars flared up between small countries; massacres decimated whole tribes. The tide of the homeless rose, visible on every street corner in New York until herded away, still cold and hungry, by the police into less visible margins of the city. Gender and sexual orientation battles rocked my society and church. You get the picture.

But I thought, *I can't save the world. What can I do?*

So many people think as I did. Isolated and alone before our newspapers or television sets, we get glimmers of a planet in trouble, though seldom the full report. In fact, the barrage of suffering that parades through our bombarded consciousness usually increases our sense of helplessness. Occasionally a big disaster hits—an earthquake, a tsunami, a hurricane—and suddenly we can do something specific. A massive outpouring follows, often of more money and material than actually needed, while other ongoing charity and development efforts are slighted, shortchanged, or ignored entirely.

In between all that suffering, commercials lure us into the consumer delights that buffer us from the harsh realities of minimum-wage workers unable to afford to rent an apartment, children killed in drive-by shootings, trees dying from acid rain, people lost in hells of their own making, and little children playing amidst the empty shells of American bombs that emit low-grade radiation.

I could go on, and so could you. The list is discouraging. What can I do? What can you do? What could the two of us even do together?

Build your life on something solid.

Everyone . . . who hears these words of mine and acts on them will be like a wise man who built his house on rock.
—MATTHEW 7:24

You can do something. You can get on a path of wisdom and walk it. A path of wisdom—practical, worldly know-how as well as deep insight into how life works best—like Jesus' path. A path he widened from the trail marked out by generations of prophets before him. A path that resonates with the insights of all the other wise trailblazers who have lived before, during, and after Jesus' earthly lifetime. "Build your house on a rock," as Jesus urges us.

This path embodies (the theological word is *incarnates*) all the ways the mysterious Love that shapes the universe has befriended the human race and desires each human's God-like potential to flourish. This path is a *halakah,* a way of living that brings blessing and challenges to help the species become more fit for this planet. Its habits of the heart and practices of daily living can shape not only the world but our souls in the life-giving ways of God. Following these practices does not *earn* salvation but rather aligns us with God's ever-available grace, the power that slowly transforms our very nature. It is God's path to true human success. The scriptures would prefer to call this "maturity" or "fruition," the full ripening of the good possibilities within the human heart.

You may ask what good all that will do in the face of a task as massive as repairing creation and building the world? I cannot offer an answer that proves the human venture on this planet will be successful in the long run. Neither did Jesus. But he encouraged his disciples not to lose heart, to trust that God's desires for the world will triumph in the end: "It is your Father's good pleasure to give you the kingdom" (Luke 12:32). Jesus explained that while the universe may sometimes seem a hard-hearted and unjust setup, persistent faith, prayer, and action will in the end prevail: "Will not God grant justice to his chosen ones who cry to him day and night?" (See Luke 18:1-8.) He said that his works of healing were small signs of the life-giving energies that would pervade the whole fabric of the world, like yeast pervades bread dough. (See Luke 11:20; Matt. 13:33.)

The Bible, from Genesis to Revelation, concerns the fate of the world more than life after death, though biblical people come to firmly believe the love and justice of God pursue us even after physical death. God is pictured putting our species on this planet to "till it and keep it" (Gen. 2:15) and trying through prophet after prophet to show people the ways that lead to peace, bounty, social harmony, and personal fulfillment. Even the faithful departed continue to pray for the full coming of the reign of God (Rev. 6:10).

Jesus, part of that line of prophets, said that the way through all difficulties was walking the path of mercy, justice, and humble cooperation with the Source of this world's life—the path he himself embodied through a process of deepening trust, hard testing, and real struggle. If we walk that way, Jesus promises, even now the kingdom can be "at hand," so close we can taste "the powers of the age to come" (Heb. 6:5), the time of full and complete triumph.

The Gospels clearly depict the disciples wavering in their willingness to trust Jesus' belief that the news from God is ultimately good. Only when the debacle of Jesus' apparent failure—his arrest and murder—was followed by experiences of his continuing power to touch lives did the disciples decide to bet their lives on Jesus' Way. Because they believed he had triumphed over injustice, evil, and death, Jesus became for them the definitive sign and seal of God's befriending the human venture, God's own *yes* to all the prophetic promises about the coming reign of justice, mercy, and peace (2 Cor. 1:20).

Okay. Okay. Promises, promises. Why should you believe such promises? Why should I?

I wondered about that for a long time in my late twenties and through the decade of my thirties. Since early adulthood I've had a deep sense that we are living at a great turning point in history, what the New Testament calls a *kairos*, a time of peril and promise. But, in spite of being a practicing Christian, I had a hard time getting hold of the promise of the kingdom's triumph.

My ears heard the words, but my heart was filled with foreboding—the same foreboding that, I fear, lies behind the pandemic of drugs and frantic diversions that blight so many lives.

Draw near to my fire.

Whoever is near me is near the fire.
—GOSPEL OF THOMAS 82

I am come to send fire on the earth.
—LUKE 12:49, KJV

Three experiences in my early forties, almost back to back, invited my whole self to believe the promise. The first took place during an Advent service of readings from the prophets.[1] The readings promised the full flowering of the world and its peoples. As I stewed about how unlikely such prophecies seemed as future scenarios, I muttered to myself, "The world really needs saving." It only took a heartbeat before I started chuckling at the irony of sitting in a church realizing the world needs saving. But for the first time the utter, raw, urgent practicality of this need became crystal clear to me. "Oh, yes," I mused. "That's what this is all about."[1]

The second experience also occurred in church, some time later, on All Saints' Day, when the heroes of all the centuries who walked the Way are celebrated. As if for the first time, I heard how the great prayer of thanksgiving in my liturgical church tells the story of God's creating the world and then befriending it in its difficulties: "When our disobedience took us far from you, you did not abandon us to the power of death. In your mercy you came to our help . . . and through the prophets you taught us to hope for salvation."[2]

"You did not abandon us." The words rang in my ears. For the first time I "got" the Good News that God cares about the human venture, wants it to succeed, is doing everything possible to help us. I was invited to trust that God alone knows the best ways through the present crisis and is working in millions of lives to bring about the kingdom.

Now, you may say, how could you have gone to church all those years and not heard those words, not believed that promise? Well, it's one thing to "believe" with some sliver of one's intellect and quite another matter for one's heart, blood, and bones to believe that such promises are real. We're called to believe and love with our whole heart, and getting that multi-chambered heart on board can be a long process, especially when some of its chambers are ruled by apprehensions and fears that loom large in any given moment. We believe and don't believe at the same time.

I didn't really say yes, however, until the third experience, which happened the next summer at a conference. The speaker was laying bare the suffering of humanity and the earth and declaring his own belief that "God so loved the world" (John 3:16) means exactly that: the world, the green-mantled planet with its myriad creatures and noble, flawed, maverick human race, not just human souls. And, earth-loving Christian that he was, he believed Jesus pointed the way to renewal and redemption for humanity and the planet. Furthermore, Jesus wanted us all as partners in the task. Evangelistically he called us to a moment of decision: Will you declare for Jesus? Will you live into the promise?

This is all desirable, I thought. *Great dream, to be sure. But how could it really come true?* Right then, something else in me or from beyond me said, quite insistently, *The only way dreams come true is if people live them. The decision is not about whether it will come true or not. The decision is about whether you think Jesus' dream is worth following or not.*

Jesus' vision of life danced before me, the prophetic dream of God's gracious rule "on earth as it is in heaven": a dream of nations that study war no more; of a time when day laborers make a living wage; when mutual affection rules community life; when souls lost in selfishness and pride turn toward humble cooperation; when healing love surrounds illness; when Spirit flows through prayer like a mighty ocean; when nature is restored to full vigor; and when death is no longer feared but recognized as the gateway to an even larger life in God's service.[3]

Everybody lives by dreams, conscious or unconscious: dreams of success or riches, love or dominance, personal privilege or devoted service; dreams of bigger homes with wrought-iron fences, a better spouse, or children to make one proud; dreams of getting even or getting it all over with. Dreams are the biggest life shapers, though we don't usually think of them that way. So it matters to which dreams we commit ourselves.

Jesus' dream for the world seemed, and seems, better to me than any other I know. So I said yes to it right there during that lecture, just as I'd said yes thirty years before to Jesus as my personal Savior when I was a teenager. God being my helper, I wanted to be part of Jesus' great task of healing souls and repairing the world.

Don't expect to be "raptured" out of this struggle.

Jesus said, "If . . . 'the kingdom is in the sky,' then the birds of the sky will get there first."
—GOSPEL OF THOMAS 3

Your kingdom come. . . . on earth as it is in heaven.
—MATTHEW 6:10

I saw the holy city, the new Jerusalem, coming down out of heaven from God, prepared as a bride adorned for her husband.
—REVELATION 21:2

Plenty of Christians would disagree with me. They're not waiting for the trees of the forest to sing for joy when the Lord comes to set things right on the earth (see Psalm 96:12-13). Quite the contrary; their bags are half-packed for liftoff, for the "rapture of the church" before the world burns to a crisp, along with the likes of me who pin our hopes on earthly things. The extremists assure themselves that environmental damage is no problem. The more the better, in fact, because it hastens the End. Then we can all—all the saved, at least—go "home."

While not all who believe in the rapture are quite so cavalier about the earth, they still have heaven on their minds. While I was in my agonizing phase—before the three experiences—I shared my distress with two truly dear and loving people at a spiritual direction training seminar. They looked a bit perplexed and even more pastorally concerned.

"But surely earth isn't the chief issue," one said. "Jesus came to save our souls." I replied that souls certainly needed saving, but that God had given the planet into our care and soul saving had something to do with the spiritual maturity needed to be the stewards of earth.

"But Bob," pleaded the other, "if that's really true, and we mess it all up, surely God will give us another home."

I don't think so. One planet per guardian species, I figure. This isn't some kind of rehearsal for the real thing we're running here in human history. This is it. This is our "home." "The heavens are the Lord's heavens, but the earth he has given to human beings" (Ps. 115:16). I don't know the true shape of the hereafter, but I do know that it's intimately connected with the here and now.

We read in the "revelation of the Lord Jesus . . . to his servant John" (Rev. 1:1) that the heavenly city descends to earth, not vice versa, renewing the whole world. (See Rev. 21:1-2.) While much of humanity seems bent on getting *out* of here to a better place, God seems intent on getting *in* here as much as possible, all the way to sharing our very flesh in the life of Jesus of Nazareth, inviting our very bodies to participate in the divine life itself.

Yearning for apocalyptic destruction and blissful rapture seems to me, with due respect, an easy way out of our God-given tasks; rather more a nightmare than a God-given dream. I may be wrong and get left behind. But I think I'll be in good company, because I can't imagine Jesus abandoning the world he lived and died to save.

Remember that I am with you always.

Remember, I am with you always.
—MATTHEW 28:20

Fortunately a significant vanguard of humanity is not looking for that kind of exit strategy. Rather they're following dreams directly based on Jesus' vision, or resonant with it, whether they know it or not. On the days when humanity seems to me to be headed into a dark tunnel, I renew myself by recalling people I know or have heard about who are conduits for the "powers of the age to come" (Heb. 6:5), the world envisioned by Jesus, signs of the divine initiative.

There are the Chuck Colsons of the world, born-again Christians whose hearts have felt the plight of some marginalized group—in Chuck's case, prisoners trapped in a nonredemptive system. He offers them "restorative justice." There are the Tony Campolos who set up inner-city schools designed solely for kids failing in the public system and the Mother Teresas who embrace dying people literally cast out on the street.

There are medical people like Dolores Krieger, Herbert Benson, Lawrence LeShan, and Dean Ornish who have brought the spiritual dimension back into health care, uniting body and spirit as Jesus did. Since all healing ultimately comes from God, these secular folk are the colleagues of Christians like Kathryn Kuhlman, Oral Roberts, Agnes Sanford, and Francis MacNutt, who have restored healing prayer to our churches.

There are secular saints like Karl Kehde, a New Jersey architect who designs eco-friendly developments, and Jacques Cousteau, who dedicated his life to awakening the love of nature in others and pointing out dire threats to the ecosystem, and many thousands whose names never appear in the newspapers.

And then there are people like those mentioned in this book: the Alices who stop drinking and stay sober in spite of opposition, the prisoners transformed by their hospice work, the Robert Johns seeking release from the prison of their anger, the Andrews who stand up to parental abuse, the Helens who put their bodies in front of earthmovers, and the nameless hundreds who pass out bottled water to the World Trade Center survivors.

All these people help me believe that we live not only in a time of peril but of promise. They show me that the divine energies I see at work in Jesus still challenge, recruit, and transform people now, in my own day.

Don't be afraid. God delights to work with you.

Fear not, little flock, for it is your Father's good pleasure to give you the Kingdom.—Luke 12:32, KJV

Ironically, convincing people that the world will end with a bang seems considerably easier than motivating them to risk a deep and committed faith in the future of the human venture and its importance to God. Weapons of mass destruction, the cracking of the genetic code, and the moral confusions of a rapidly changing world provide easy fodder for the failure of nerve on which apocalypticism feeds.

Jesus, as we have seen, faced this very problem in his own ministry. Every time he caught his disciples looking to the sky in hopes the sudden coming of the kingdom would swoop in and rescue them, he pointed them to their lives and responsibilities here and now. Now, here, in this place, the energies of God's reign are at work. "It is not for you to know the times or periods that the Father has set by his own authority" (Acts 1:7). Jesus told many stories about the delay of the Master's return, and he encouraged everyday faithfulness to the kingdom's energies, urging his disciples not to lose faith though the time seemed long.[4]

I do not know how long it will take for God's reign to come in its fullness. The New Testament indicates that Jesus refused to set out a timetable and may even have changed his own expectations about the final coming of the kingdom as his ministry proceeded.[5] But I do know that the vision of Jesus and the Way of Jesus call me not to be disheartened, no matter how dangerous the meandering, staggering way of history may be. Say it's all the stuff of dreams, if you wish. As I've said, we all live by dreams, and I want to live by a dream that serves the good of the earth that gave me flesh, the God who loved that earth into being, and the best potentials that dwell at the heart of human nature.

So my final dream—or vision or parable—is one that came to me in the middle of a dark night when I was wrestling with myself, the world, and God for some hope in the future.

I saw that the present moment in history (and, in fact, all of history) resembles the whole human race going down a mighty river, through perilous white water, in a large flotilla of rafts. The creative Intelligence that called us to this journey sits at the back of the biggest raft. Ancient beyond reckoning yet somehow fresh and young, with strength to hold the rudder as steady as possible in the churning waters that buffet and rock the raft to and fro, this divine pilot is like the calm at the center of a storm, alert and in touch with every movement of the flotilla, like a great animal attuned to its surroundings.

We're all jammed into the rafts, cheek by jowl, some of us sitting perilously close to the raging waters, all of us getting wet from the spray. Not only this generation but every generation that ever lived, somehow, is there. Maybe because the ancestors are implicit in our genes. Or maybe they peek out through our souls from their place of prayer and labor for God's purposes. They care deeply about whether their life efforts will keep on bearing fruit into the human future. They know that without us, the living, their own labors for the good of God's earth can never come to full fruition. (See Heb. 11:40.) These past generations pray that we will stay true to the task of loving the world into fuller and richer being.

Every once in a while it seems like we won't make it. We hit terrible rapids that almost swamp the rafts. Each time that happens, God speaks softly, strongly, comfortingly, encouragingly: "Hang on. Keep paddling. Everything will be all right." Like a rider reassuring a nervous horse on the edge of bolting, like a captain rallying the troops, like Jesus giving the disciples hope just before his betrayal and death, or like a mother humming to quiet her infant while danger stalks all around her, God speaks soothing, encouraging, strengthening words to us.

Dare we trust this voice, which whispers like a breath deep inside us, raising hope in spite of dark headlines, inviting us to follow its lead into the future? We can't know for a certainty, of course, till we get to where the Voice points us, just as Moses was told he'd know the Exodus was a success only when it succeeded. (See Exod. 3:12.) But every time an individual or group decides to follow his Way, some aspect of Jesus walks again on this earth.

Jesus' ultimate challenge to us—the provocation behind all other challenges—is this: we can decide to have faith in God's venture among us or not. In every life, in every generation, however much or little of this wisdom we have learned, that is the choice.

On our decision angels, ancestors, and all our descendants as well wait with bated breath.

QUESTIONS FOR REFLECTION AND DISCUSSION

1. What human attitudes and actions make you doubtful about the world's future? What gives you hope about humanity's venture on this planet? How do you think God is involved in shaping the future?

2. This book claims God is saving the world, not just human souls. How does this claim challenge or confirm your current beliefs? What place does planet earth have in God's plans?

3. "Dare we trust this voice, which whispers like a breath deep inside us, raising hope in spite of the latest dark headlines, inviting us to follow its lead into the future?" In what ways do the teaching of Jesus and the visions of the biblical prophets invite us to "trust this voice"?

A Note about Biblical Scholarship

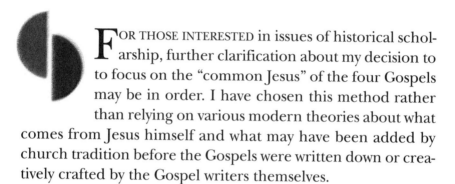

FOR THOSE INTERESTED in issues of historical scholarship, further clarification about my decision to to focus on the "common Jesus" of the four Gospels may be in order. I have chosen this method rather than relying on various modern theories about what comes from Jesus himself and what may have been added by church tradition before the Gospels were written down or creatively crafted by the Gospel writers themselves.

THE GOSPEL TEXTS AND THE "REAL JESUS"

Let me state clearly that while I am no fundamentalist about the Gospel texts, I am deeply skeptical about attempts to get behind the text to the "real Jesus." I accept fully that each Evangelist arranges sayings and stories from the oral tradition to address issues important to his first-century community. The similarities and differences between the three Synoptic ("having the same eye") Gospels—Matthew, Mark, and Luke—illustrate this decisively. The same saying often ends up in very different contexts in these Gospels. It is hard to avoid the conclusion that the four Gospels are historical memory shaped by later reflection and illumination.

The discovery of long-lost texts of other Gospels in the twentieth century, especially the Gospel of Thomas, reveals how the sayings tradition diversified in various first-century communities where Jesus' words were remembered. Matthew's Jesus speaks as a second Moses; Mark's, as the Spirit-possessed Son of Man;

Luke's, as a healer, prophet, and social reformer; John's, as a mystic in union with God; and Thomas's, as a mystic illuminator.

An entire scholarly art has evolved in order to determine which sayings are authentic and which ones are products of the second-generation church. Furthermore, more than a few scholars have come to feel that the second-generation church substantially misunderstood the original Jesus, making him Messiah, for example, when he made no such claim.

As refined a scholarly discipline as this may be, it is still guess-work, based on little actual evidence and inevitably influenced by the presuppositions of the scholar. All we have about Jesus is the memory of him in the community that began with the disciples during his ministry. No outside witnesses. No other historical records. The Jesus of the Gospel texts is the only Jesus, historically speaking, that we have. No other first-century texts worth mentioning exist.[1]

Much modern biblical scholarship operates under a hermeneutic of suspicion: every story or saying in the Gospels is doubtful until proven authentic. Perhaps I am invincibly naive, but I believe historical texts should be considered innocent till proven guilty. I know carefully devised rules apply to these scholarly decisions: multiple attestation, for example, suggests a greater probability of authenticity than one lone citing. While such proof may make sense in a court of law, I'm not sure how close to real life it comes. I, like anybody else, say some things only to a trusted friend; other things quite publicly. After my death, that lone witness would still be telling the truth.

Likewise, differences in style and vocabulary are used as criteria for authenticity. Certainly we all have characteristic styles of speaking but often more than one. I know more than one mystically inclined person, for example, who speaks quite differently when describing a transcendent experience than in ordinary conversation. The mystical rhetoric of John's Jesus diverges from the pithy proverbs and peppery prose of the Synoptic Jesus, to be sure; and Jesus' speeches in John may have been influenced by post-Resurrection experiences of illumination from the "living Christ." But the man Jesus in mystic rapture may have spoken quite differently than the public preacher, and the long speeches in John may indeed have historical roots.

Finally, assumptions about the development of doctrine influence decisions about authenticity and historicity. Passages with high Christology—presenting Jesus as charged with divinity or asserting a mystical unity with God—often are deemed signs of "later church reflection."

All the presuppositions above are imposed upon the text. As the scholarly history of the last two-and-a-half centuries shows, presuppositions change constantly. What one considers authentic depends heavily on what seems plausible, and plausibilities change. Knowledge about the ancient world expands, and new likelihoods emerge.

Transpersonal and depth psychology make the dreams and visions of the Gospels more plausible than did nineteenth- and early-twentieth-century rationalistic psychology. The revival of spiritual healing and the new interest in mind-body medicine make the Gospel healing stories more plausible than they seemed to many a century ago. Comparative religion gives us stories of transfigurations from the lives of holy men of other faiths and may make the story of a man shining with light more plausible. The discovery of the Dead Sea Scrolls, new studies in intertestamental apocalypticism and second-Temple Jewish mysticism make a man claiming an exalted relation with God more plausible.[2] The scrolls also reveal a pre-Christian example of a highly organized brotherhood with sacramental meals, councils of twelve, even "overseers," making more plausible a Jesus who sets in place the foundations of a fellowship that became the Christian church.

Nothing in all this analysis proves how historically reliable the Gospels are or that all the sayings attributed to Jesus came from his own mouth; nor does any of it disprove reliability. That is my point. There's virtually no way to know for sure.

Likewise, I do not see why we should find the Jesus in the recently discovered alternative or Gnostic (from *gnosis*, mystical knowledge) Gospels as more authentic than the man reported by the traditional Gospels, as some would have us do.[3] I'm inclined to accept these other Gospels as fascinating witnesses to the impression Jesus' words made in people's lives and the way their meaning was developed. I feel they may help us understand the traditional Gospels better. They certainly demonstrate that a division of opinion grew up in the church about what aspect of Jesus' words was most important—the communal and sacramental or the mystical and illuminative, for example.

But I see no way to determine that the Jesus of the Gospel of Thomas or Mary or Phillip is more authentic than the Jesus of Matthew, Mark, Luke, and John. Just because the part of the church that came to call itself "orthodox" won the battle for power in early Christianity doesn't mean it was wrong about everything! The sad fact is that, in the bitter battle between mystical experience and church authority, the early Christian mystical "baby" was too often thrown out with the Gnostic "bathwater." So, I say, let the Gnostic Gospels be commentary on the canonical Gospels, not replacements.

As stated in the Introduction, I side with the "common Jesus" of the last two thousand years because the Jesus of the Gospel texts is the one with the most massive weight of historical influence through the centuries. This figure is the most likely to continue to prevail in history. I would rather let the alternative material illuminate the canonical texts than substitute the Jesus there for the Jesus who continues to shape the lives of most Christians. Used this way, these other texts enrich our picture of Jesus—and make it more paradoxical.

Because I am not an academically credentialed New Testament scholar (I possess no PhD in New Testament studies, only a postgraduate seminary degree), the reader may freely disregard my opinions as the passions of a mere academic layperson.

Though a nonexpert, I have read widely and deeply in the scholarly literature—conservative, liberal, and radical—since before my seminary training. I'm grateful for all the historical information that much of this scholarship has surfaced and presented.

But all attempts to trim the rough and sometimes contradictory witness of early Christian texts down to a consistent version of Jesus threaten to make him less complex than any of us. The man wants to rattle our cages and provoke us out of comfortable social or religious conformities into the exciting and frightening freedom of adult response to God. Speculation about authorship, origins, and authenticity can too easily blunt the disarming effect of the full range of sayings attributed to this man. May these provocative words never cease to challenge and disturb the waking life of humanity.

"Apprentices of the Master" Project

Which of Jesus' sayings challenges you most right now in your life? How are you living it out right now? What are the difficulties? the successes? How is exploring this challenge stretching and maturing you in your spiritual journey?

The *"Apprentices of the Master" Project* provides an Internet space where discoveries, experiences, and questions may be shared. Each month a fresh saying will be posted, with background commentary provided by Robert Corin Morris. A threaded conversation will allow you to read and respond to what others are discovering in their own spiritual practice.

The purpose is simple: to create the opportunity for frank sharing about how the words of Jesus are alive and shaping lives today. For further information, go to the Interweave Web site: www.interweave.org/apprentices, e-mail the project at apprentices@interweave.org, or write "Apprentices of the Master" Project, c/o Interweave, P.O. Box 1516, Summit, NJ 07901.

Notes

Introduction: Looking for a Fresh Vision of Jesus

1. In popular fiction, Dan Brown's *The Da Vinci Code* (New York, Doubleday, 2002) leads the pack of canonical Gospel debunkers, claiming the church hid the fact of Jesus' marriage to Mary Magdalene and suppressed his real teachings. On a scholarly level, the work of the famous Jesus Seminar claims to be able to distinguish the authentic sayings of Jesus from the overlay of second-generation interpretation. See *The Five Gospels: The Search for the Authentic Words of Jesus: New Translation and Commentary,* edited by Robert W. Funk, Roy W. Hoover, and the Jesus Seminar (New York: Macmillan, 1993). For a positive angle of the value of this scholarship for faith, see Marcus J. Borg, *Meeting Jesus Again for the First Time: The Historical Jesus and the Heart of Contemporary Faith* (San Francisco: HarperSanFrancisco, 1994).

The "alternative" or noncanonical Gospels recovered during the past century include the Gospels of Thomas, Mary (Magdalene), and Philip. See James. M. Robinson, ed., *The Nag Hammadi Library in English* (New York: Harper & Row, 1988). For a study that claims these Gospels represent a more authentic version of Jesus, see Elaine Pagels, *The Gnostic Gospels* (New York: Vintage/Random House, 1981). For a parallel arrangement of Gospel texts that includes the noncanonical material, see Robert Funk, *New Gospel Parallels,* Foundations and Facets Series (Philadelphia: Fortress Press, 1985).

2.   Orthodox Christianity holds that Jesus is "fully human and fully divine," but teachings through the years have varied, some emphasizing humanity and others divinity. See especially J. N. D. Kelly, "The Beginnings of Christology," chapter 6 in *Early Christian Doctrines* (New York: Harper & Brothers, 1959), 138–63.

3.   Abraham argues with God over the fate of Sodom and Gomorrah (Gen. 18:17-33), and Moses argues God out of wrathful outbursts against the people of Israel (Deut. 12:9-29). Rabbinical stories abound about God in debate with the angels and with human beings. See Rabbi Bradley N. Bleefeld and Robert L. Shook, *Saving the World Entire: And 100 Other Beloved Parables from the Talmud* (New York: Plume/Penguin, 1998).

4.   I do not question the endeavor to rank the Gospels in chronological order, with Mark as the earliest, nor to discern the building blocks that went into the Gospels. I do question whether the earliest automatically qualifies as most reliable. Early church tradition says, for example, that John knew Matthew, Mark, and Luke, and wrote his Gospel to include material left out of them. See *Eusebius: The History of the Church from Christ to Constantine,* trans. G. A. Williamson (New York: Dorset Press, 1965), section 24, 131–34.

5.   For an informed tour of the repeated cycles of New Testament scholarship, see Charlotte Allen, *The Human Christ: The Search for the Historical Jesus* (New York: The Free Press, 1998).

Chapter 1
Jesus the Provocateur

Portions of chapter 1 first appeared as "Enlightening Annoyances: Jesus' Teachings as a Spur to Spiritual Growth," in *Weavings* 16, no. 5 (September /October 2001) and in Robert Corin Morris, *Wrestling with Grace: A Spirituality for the Rough Edges of Daily Life* (Nashville, Tenn.: Upper Room Books, 2003), chap. 4.

1.   Support in offering hospitality to an important guest was often a matter of community honor. Jesus refers to this social reality when he says, "Suppose one of you has a friend, and you go to him at midnight and say to him, 'Friend, lend me three loaves of bread; for a friend of mine has arrived.'" See Luke 11:5-8.

2.   The exilic prophet Ezekiel announces a major change in the law: no longer will families be punished for the sins of an individual (Ezek. 18). Jesus repeatedly declares legal regulation secondary to pressing human need: sabbath regulations can be overruled to heal the sick or even satisfy the hunger of the disciples (Mark 2:23-28). Traditional Jewish law, rooted in the same era, also recognizes that human need can, on occasion, take precedence over legal strictures. For example: "On Sabbath a man should always walk with an easy and leisurely gait, but to do a good act...a man should always run, even on Sabbath." (C. G. Montefiore and H. Loewe, *A Rabbinic Anthology* [Cleveland, Ohio: Meridian Books, 1963], 194).

3.   Sayings need to be seen against the historical background of Jesus' day. It is likely that Jesus' advice to turn the other cheek and to go the "extra mile" if compelled by a soldier refer to the situation of foreign occupation. They are counsels to a powerless population against acts of retaliation that will only bring more trouble down on the individual or community, not maxims for all situations.

4.   For a description of the community of the Scrolls, see Willis Barnstone, ed., *The Other Bible: Ancient Esoteric Texts from the Pseudepigrapha, the Dead Sea Scrolls, the Early Kabbalah, the Nag Hammadi Library and Other Sources* (San Francisco: Harper & Row, 1984). Many scholars identify the Essenes with the Scroll Community, which may have lived at Qumran near the Dead Sea in monastic seclusion, and believed, as did Jesus and Paul, that the "one flesh" of marriage is meant to be indissoluble.

5.   The New Testament is clear that Jesus faced the dark side of human nature in his own experience, able to "sympathize

with our weaknesses" because he "has been tested as we are." See Heb. 4:15, as well as 2:14-18. To say he came through these tests "without sin" does not necessarily imply the man never made a mistake but rather that he remained devoted to finding and following God's way through all of it. Jesus himself never claimed absolute human perfection, but rather said, "Why do you call me good? No one is good but God alone" (Mark 10:18).

6.   Roman Catholics forbid divorce but allow annulment and remarriage. Eastern Orthodox recognize the "spiritual death" of a marriage as allowing remarriage. Most Protestants now take the teaching as an ideal but "pastorally understand" the necessity of divorce and allow remarriage with the church's blessing.

7.   Christians need to recognize that historical Judaism does not see obedience to the Torah as a burdensome list of regulations. Both Christianity and Judaism have had their legalists. Certain strands of Judaism, especially Hasidism, see *halakah* as a path of loving response to God.

8.   *Yoke* and *yoga* are from the common Sanskrit root *-yueg*. See William Morris, ed., *The American Heritage Dictionary* (New York: Houghton Mifflin, 1969). The yoke symbol became common in Jewish circles for the discipline of learning wisdom: "Her yoke is a golden ornament," says Ben Sirach (Sirach 6:30).

9.   *Teleo* is related to *telos*, the "end" or "fulfillment." Saint Jerome uses the Latin *perfecti* to translate this in the Vulgate, a term that refers to someone who has finished a course of training or initiation, a person proficient in a craft or area of knowledge.

Chapter 2
Transform Your Heart and Mind

1.   Practicing Jews characteristically avoid direct reference to God, to prevent taking the Divine name in vain. They substitute "the Name" or "heaven" or as Jesus himself says, "the

Majesty." Hence, the kingdom of "heaven" is kingdom of God, not a kingdom located in heaven.

2.   Many of Jesus' sayings are styled as utterances of the divine Wisdom itself, either directly quoting or adapting statements from the "sapiential" literature found in Proverbs and deuterocanonical books like the Wisdom of Solomon, the Wisdom of Jesus ben Sirach, and Esdras, from which the "like a hen gathers her brood" metaphor may be drawn (2 Esdras 1:30). Pithy proverbs from these works were apparently in wide circulation in the culture of Jesus' day. In this literature, Wisdom is seen as an "emanation" of the Divine, personified as a feminine figure, who is God's collaborator in creation and the providential care of humankind. This exalted heavenly figure stands behind the "high" Christology of Paul's letters and the Gospel of John, where Jesus is seen as the embodiment of the eternal Wisdom or Word of God. The source of this may be Jesus' own identification of himself as the representative of Wisdom in his sayings. See Margaret Barker, *The Great Angel: Israel's Second God* (Louisville, Ky.: Westminster John Knox Press, 1992).

3.   *Metanoia* in Greek means, literally, "beyond (*meta*) mind (*noia*)," which I take to mean a transformation of consciousness. The emphasis on the interiority of a changed mind in repentance is new in Second Temple Judaism, and an old Hebrew word, *teshuvah*, meaning "return," comes to be used by the rabbis for this process of inner turning toward God. "Repent," on the other hand, derives from the Latin word for punishment (*poena*) and means "to regret or be sorry," which shifts the emphasis away from God and a return to the path of goodness toward our own remorse.

4.   Some theologians make a sharper distinction between *agape* and *eros*. For a classic treatment of a sharp distinction, see Anders Nygren, *Agape and Eros* (Chicago: University of Chicago Press, 1982).

5.   Even in Mark 13, when Jesus outlines the usual apocalyptic signs of the impending kingdom, he says "the end is still

to come" (v. 7) and warns the disciples to beware of being led astray by sign-gazers. Jesus did not so much reject other expectations as emphasize the existential *now* as the crucial ingredient in realizing any other aspect of the kingdom, personal or political, present or future.

6.   Jesus and John the Baptist can be seen as the prophets of the destruction of the Second Temple in 70 CE as Jeremiah and Ezekiel were for the First Temple's fall in 586 BCE. See Scot McKnight, *A New Vision for Israel: The Teachings of Jesus in National Context* (Grand Rapids, Mich.: Wm. B. Eerdmans Publishing Co., 1999). Jesus' declaration that those who take the sword will perish by the sword (Matt. 26:52) defines his dissent from the Zealots who were preparing for the disastrous armed rebellion that broke out in 66 CE and led to the destruction of Jerusalem and the Temple and resulted in two thousand years of Jewish exile among the nations.

7.   Jesus' famous statement about entering the kingdom as a child is, like so much else, an open invitation to exploration. Common interpretations focus on a childlike, trusting faith. What catches my imagination is the inquisitive gaze of the child who has not yet labeled and categorized reality but remains open to fresh encounter. In Thomas the image symbolizes both consciousness free from shame and innocence combined with ancient wisdom. See the Gospel of Thomas, Logia 4 and 37.

Chapter 3
Remove the Hindrances to Love

1.   "Louisiana Prison Hospice," in *Religion and Ethics Weekly*, Episode no. 339, May 26, 2000. For information about this program, see Web site: www.pbs.org/wnet/religionandethics.

2.   For information about Archbishop Tutu and forgiveness, see Web site of The Forgiveness Project: www.theforgivenessproject.com/stories/desmond-tutu

3.   For more information about the relationship of forgiveness and heart health, see Dean Ornish, *Love and Survival: The*

Scientific Basis for the Healing Power of Intimacy (New York: Harper-Collins, 1998).

4.   The outbreak of violent conflict between Jews and Arabs in the British Protectorate of Palestine began in 1929 with the massacre of Jews in Hebron, rose to new heights in the Israeli War of Independence in 1947–49, and has continued since.

Chapter 4
Put God's Priorities First

1.   The Hebrew prophets are consistent in denouncing the neglect of the poor by the socially advantaged. The eighth-century BCE prophet Amos is characteristic: "Hear this, you that trample on the needy, and bring to ruin the poor of the land, saying, 'When will the new moon be over so that we may sell grain; and the sabbath, so that we may offer wheat for sale? We will make the ephah small and the shekel great, and practice deceit with false balances, buying the poor for silver and the needy for a pair of sandals, and selling the sweepings of the wheat.' The LORD has sworn by the pride of Jacob: Surely I will never forget any of their deeds" (Amos 8:4-7).

2.   Psalm 72 says that a king true to God will "defend the cause of the poor of the people, give deliverance to the needy" (v. 4). He "has pity on the weak . . . and saves the lives of the needy" (v. 13). This seems to establish an incontestable biblical principle that government has a responsibility to provide a safety net for the poor and handicapped. The Temple also provided alms for the poor.

3.   Mark 1:20 ("They left their father Zebedee in the boat with the hired men") indicates that this was a business successful enough to have hired men.

4.   "Practice of charity" is listed in morning meditations among the "things the fruits of which a man enjoys in this world, while the stock remains for him in the world to come." Dr. A. Th. Philips, *Daily Prayers with English Translation*, rev. ed. (New York: Hebrew Publishing Company, n.d.), Morning Service, 19, 21.

5.   See "Caesar and Christ: Taming the Pecking Order," chapter 13, in Robert Corin Morris, *Wrestling with Grace: A Spirituality for the Rough Edges of Daily Life* (Nashville: Upper Room Books, 2003), especially 156–57.

6.   The Greek word *psyche,* translated "soul" in the King James Version, is now often translated as "life." It means both identity and vitality.

7.   See Frederick Douglass, *Narrative of the Life of Frederick Douglass, an American Slave,* in *Frederick Douglass: Autobiographies* (New York: Library of America, 1996), chapter 6.

Chapter 5
Practice God's Family Values

1.   In the pragmatic sense of the commandment, "honoring father and mother" means supporting them in old age, maintaining social customs that will keep each generation supporting the preceding one: "so that your days may be long" (Deut. 5:16). Jesus inveighs against diverting funds meant to support aging parents to *korban,* Temple investment accounts, technically removing them from the family resources (Matt. 15:5-6).

2.   The Greek word for hate, *miseo,* can be translated as "aversion."

3.   The family of Jesus is remembered by the early church as exercising considerable influence in the first generation. Mary and the brothers are present with the disciples before Pentecost (Acts 1:14); brother James is among those graced with a vision of the risen Lord (1 Cor. 15:7). The brothers (and sisters) are variously considered to be children of Mary and Joseph or Joseph's children by a previous marriage. According to the early church historian Eusebius, the kinsmen of Jesus continued to be consulted in making important decisions. See G. A. Williamson, trans., Eusebius, *The History of the Church from Christ to Constantine* (New York: Dorset Press, 1965), sect. 11.1, p. 123.

4.   Something like the modern world's passionate drive for personal autonomy and self-realization was not completely alien

to the ancient world. The Gospel of Thomas links personal self-realization, becoming "solitary," or *monakhos*, with separation from the power of family: "For five people will be in a house: it will be three against two and two against three, father against son and son against father, and they will stand alone" (Marvin W. Meyer, trans. *The Secret Teachings of Jesus: Four Gnostic Gospels* [New York: Vintage Books, 1986], 22). Our word *monk* derives from *monokos*.

5.   For a brilliant analysis in the light of depth psychology and liberation theology of the New Testament's language about the fallen angelic powers that stand behind human institutions, see Walter Wink's Powers series: *Naming the Powers: The Language of Power in the New Testament* (1984); *Unmasking the Powers: The Invisible Forces That Determine Human Existence* (1986); *Engaging the Powers: Discernment and Resistance in a World of Domination* (1992), all published by Fortress Press, Minneapolis.

6.   The Greek word *martyr*, "witness," comes to mean one who witnesses to the point of death because of the execution of so many early Christians for alleged treason against the state.

Chapter 6
Practice Simple Justice

1.   See a compilation of different versions of the Golden Rule at: www.jcu.edu/philosophy/gensler/goldrule.htm.

2.   See Web site cited in note 1.

3.   Manners are quite important to some biblical Wisdom writers, especially to Jesus ben Sirach, author of the deutero-canonical book traditionally dubbed Ecclesiasticus by Christians, the "church book," because it was so prized by the early church. It is part of scripture for Roman Catholics and Orthodox, and read in services by Anglicans and some Lutherans. Examples of this concern include "Do not refrain from speaking at the proper moment" (Sirach 4:23); "Do not be like a lion in your home" (4:30); "Do not boast about wearing fine clothes" (11:4); and "Do not reprove your neighbor at a banquet" (31:31).

4.   Rowan Williams, *Lost Icons: Reflections on Cultural Bereavement* (Edinburgh: T&T Clark, 2000), 58.

5.   See Robert Corin Morris, *Wrestling with Grace*, 63–68.

Chapter 7
Welcome the Stranger

Portions of chapter 7 appeared as "Fear or Fascination? God's Call in a Multicultural World" in *Weavings* 18, no. 5 (September/October 2003):15–22.

1.   Some would limit Jesus' meaning of the "least of these" brothers and sisters to the apostles themselves. Jesus represents God; the apostles represent Jesus; to refuse to treat the disciples well is an insult to God. The New Revised Standard Version of the Bible, for example, often translates "brother" as "member of the church." The translation is not, technically, incorrect, but I feel such a narrowing of interpretation misses the wonderful ambiguities of Jesus' characteristic both/and rhetoric. The disciples represent God, yes, but on behalf of a message that everyone is to be treated as a child of God. In any case, the traditional interpretation has been to see every needy person as Christ in disguise.

2.   The Jesus Seminar, for example, tends to see "Son of Man" as a declaration of simple humanity, as does John Dominic Crossan in *The Historical Jesus: The Life of a Mediterranean Jewish Peasant* (San Francisco: HarperSanFranciso, 1991).

3.   Proverbs 25:21 says, "If your enemies are hungry, give them bread to eat." See the section about hospitality in Morris S. Seale, *The Desert Bible: Nomadic Culture and Old Testament Interpretation* (New York: St. Martin's Press, 1974), 123–26.

4.   John 4 seems to indicate that a community accepting Jesus' Way predates his death. Acts 8:14 lists Samaria as one of the first places to accept the post-Resurrection proclamation of the kingdom.

5.   Matthew 10:5-6 pictures Jesus sending his disciples only

to the "lost sheep of the house of Israel" (Matt. 15:24), and, quite specifically, not to any Samaritan village. Other Gospels report trips through Samaria. Jesus likewise tells a Canaanite woman he will not help her because he is sent only to the "lost sheep of the house of Israel," only to reverse his stance and heal her daughter because of the woman's intense faith. Such stories may indicate a gradual change in Jesus' own consciousness toward fuller acceptance of non-Jews.

6.   I believe this is a deliberate political strategy on Jesus' part. He sees his followers as the paradigm for a renewed Israel which will be as inclusive as God's own heart. As he tells the twelve: "you . . . will also sit on twelve thrones, judging the twelve tribes of Israel" (Matt. 19:28).

7.   The Pharisaic movement had enlarged the meaning of the Torah's ritual uncleanness proscriptions. Most of these rules were originally intended to apply to entering ritually holy space. The Pharisees, in their ardent zeal to sanctify ordinary daily life, said the Temple regulations about purity applied everywhere in the land of Israel.

8.   See www.studycircles.com—Study Circle Resource Center.

Chapter 8
Trust that the News is Ultimately Good

1.   For citations about mercy and wrath in rabbinical teaching, see Montefiore and Loewe, *A Rabbinic Anthology*, 233–71.

Jesus' descent into Hades between his crucifixion and resurrection became a favorite topic for Christian iconography and art, especially in the Middle Ages. It offered a hopeful edge to otherwise terrifying paintings of the wicked being tortured in hell. Eastern Orthodoxy emphasizes Christ's release of Adam and Eve from the prison-house of death, a sign of the potential redemption of all that are "in Adam."

3.   Belief that God's determination to save souls will finally triumph for all was widespread in postapostolic Christianity, hell

being considered a place of purification, not eternal doom. The great second-century philosopher-theologians Origen and Clement, both of Alexandria, and fourth-century spiritual giant Gregory of Nyssa all believed in the *apocatastasis,* or "renewal of all things," of which Jesus speaks. The Fourth Ecumenical Council in Constantinople (553) resisted efforts by the Emperor Justinian to condemn this teaching. This vision of "all things . . . being brought to their perfection" (The Book of Common Prayer [New York: The Seabury Press, 1979], 528) is rooted in Jewish visions of a world restored and repaired by the love of God.

4.   See Isaiah 10:5, where the prophet sees the hated Assyrians as the "rod" of God's anger against Israel and Judah. The Second Isaiah understands the Persian King Cyrus as God's anointed one, unknowing as the military leader may be of his part in the divine purposes (see Isa. 45:1-13).

Chapter 9
Be Partners in My Work

1.   For more information about the Partners with God training workshops write Interweave, P.O. Box 1516, Summit, NJ 07901, or e-mail Interweave through its Web site, www.inter weave.org. The program includes a forty-eight-page workbook, *Nourishing Spirituality in Congregations,* by Robert Corin Morris and Tilly-Jo Emerson (Summit, N.J.: Interweave, 1999), which may be ordered separately.

2.   Elisha recalled an apparently dead boy to life by lying on top of his body and breathing for a very long time into his mouth (2 Kings 4:32-37). Jesus is reported to have raised people from the dead with a touch and commanding words. (See Mark 5:35-43; Luke 7:11-16.) Jesus himself says that Jairus' daughter is in a death coma: "The child is not dead but sleeping" (Mark 5:39).

3.   *Suffering and the Courage of God: Exploring How Grace and Suffering Meet* (Brewster, Massachusetts: Paraclete, 2005).

4.   For a basic books on healing in a Christian context, see Avery Brooke, *Healing in the Landscape of Prayer* (Cambridge: Cowley Press, 1996), and Agnes Mary White Sanford, *The Healing Light* (St. Paul, Minn.: Macalester Park Publishing Co., 1949). For a summary of medical research into healing prayer, see Larry Dossey, *Healing Words: The Power of Prayer and the Practice of Medicine* (San Francisco: HarperSanFrancisco, 1993).

5.   For the debate about Jesus' connection to the Zealot movement, see S. G. F. Brandon, *Jesus and the Zealots: A Study of the Political Factor in Primitive Christianity* (New York: Scribner, 1967), and Oscar Cullmann, *Jesus and the Revolutionaries*, trans. Gareth Putnam (New York: Harper & Row, 1970).

6.   While the primary meaning of "take up your cross" seems to be social and political, the phrase has also been understood to cover any kind of suffering borne redemptively. See Morris, *Suffering and the Courage of God*, chapter 1.

7.   Modern liberation movements like abolition and women's rights are often taught from a purely secular standpoint, as if humanist ethics were the major driving force. Christian involvement in these movements has been pivotal. For a quick overview of the power of religion in American politics and culture, see R. Laurence Moore, *Touchdown Jesus: The Mixing of Sacred and Secular in American History* (Louisville, Ky.: Westminster John Knox Press, 2003).

8.   For the history of creation by Wisdom, see Proverbs 8:22-31. For the story of Israel retold with Wisdom as the providential aspect of God at work, see The Wisdom of Solomon 7:22–12:22.

9.   This connection with Wisdom gives rise to Jesus' statement "No one comes to the father but by me," which follows "I am the way" (John 14:6). That is, the wisdom Jesus manifests— love and forgiveness, justice and mercy, courage and faithfulness—is, by its very nature, the only way to come to the God whose very nature is these virtues. The Way is not confined to the historical Jesus; rather, Jesus manifests fully the Way, many elements of which have been taught by other spiritual teachers.

Chapter 10
Do Not Lose Heart

1.   See Morris, *Wrestling with Grace*, 115–16.

2.   "Eucharistic Prayer D," in The Book of Common Prayer, 373.

3.   The Gospels report Jesus' affirmation of the main lines of prophetic vision. War will cease (Isa. 2:4; Mic. 4:3; Matt. 26:52). The poor will be supported and treated fairly (Isa. 14:30; Zech. 3:10; Matt. 20:1-16). Humanity turns away from conflict to cooperation (Isa. 11:1-13; Luke 13:29; Rev. 21:24; 22:2). Healing energies abound (Isa. 35:6; Luke 7:22). God's presence fills all things like an ocean (Isa. 11:9). Nature is restored to full vigor (Ps. 96:11-13). Death is a gateway to larger life (Isa. 25:7-8; John 11:25-26).

4.   Matthew 24–25, especially, contain parables about the delay of the Master's return. Some scholars attribute these tales to the second-generation church as it realized the present world order was not about to end as quickly as had been hoped. I wonder, however, if these stories are not rooted in Jesus' own teachings about the delay of the kingdom for so many decades and centuries in Israel's life. They would then naturally have been applied later to his own return as Son of Man and the ultimate triumph of the kingdom.

5.   The Gospels report Jesus saying the messengers he is sending out "will not have gone through all the towns of Israel before the Son of Man comes" (Matt. 10:23), indicating an impending triumph of God's reign. Another saying claims that the kingdom will have come fully before the apostles die (Mark 9:1). A saying later in Mark's Gospel (13:10) has it that the "good news must first be proclaimed to all nations" before the full dawning of God's reign. Do these sayings represent different opinions in the early church or Jesus' own dawning realization that the kingdom he perceives as so near is not taking hold for others as urgently and quickly? Jesus' prayer in the garden of

Gethsemane also may suggest he had not begun his ministry expecting its apparent failure to turn the nation in his direction.

Afterword
A Note about Biblical Scholarship

1.   There is a reference to Jesus and his disciples in the "Slavonic Additions" to the ancient Jewish historian Josephus's *The Jewish War,* almost universally rejected as later Christian interpolations by scholars. Likewise, the Jewish Talmud mentions a Jesus and his followers, but the name was common, and the reference claims this Jesus was stoned to death for blasphemy. Other than occasional mention of Christians in official Roman documents, the only records of the first century and a half of Christian life come from the early Church itself.

2.   For a fascinating challenge to the assumption that the Nicene Creed derives from a long process of elevation of Jesus to divinity, see Margaret Barker, *The Great Angel: A Study of Israel's Second God* (Louisville, Ky.: Westminster John Knox Press, 1992) and *The Risen Lord: The Jesus of History as the Christ of Faith* (Valley Forge, Pa.: Trinity Press International, 1997).

3.   Elaine Pagels has been a leading proponent of a more authentic Jesus to be found in the Gnostic texts. For a moving account of her personal journey toward this view, see *Beyond Belief: The Secret Gospel of Thomas* (New York: Random House, 2003). I personally feel Dr. Pagels draws too sharp a contrast between Thomas and the Gospel of John, which has an understanding of *gnosis* she misses.

For Further Reading

This is a purely personal sampling of books I have found particularly helpful for myself and for people in the classes I teach. They represent a variety of views on New Testament scholarship and related subjects.

Allen, Charlotte. *The Human Christ: The Search for the Historical Jesus.* New York: The Free Press, 1998. A detailed overview of the recurrent cycles of skepticism and renewed respect for biblical historicity in Gospel scholarship since the mid-1700s.

Barker, Margaret. *The Great Angel: A Study of Israel's Second God* Louisville, Ky.: Westminster John Knox Press, 1992. *The Risen Lord: The Jesus of History as the Christ of Faith.* Valley Forge, Pa.: Trinity Press International, 1997. Grounded in extensive intertestamental material, Barker argues that the New Testament world of symbols is deeply rooted in the old Israelite religion and that the idea of Jesus as divine or semidivine is from Jewish, not Hellenistic, roots.

Barnstone, Willis. *The Other Bible: Ancient Esoteric Texts from the Pseudepigrapha, the Dead Sea Scrolls, the Early Kabbala, the Nag Hammadi Library and Other Sources.* San Francisco: Harper & Row, 1984. An accessible anthology of selections from non-canonical texts in the early years of the Christian movement.

Bleefeld, Rabbi Bradley N. and Robert L. Shook. *Saving the World Entire: And 100 Other Beloved Parables from the Talmud.*

New York: Plume/Penguin, 1998. A wonderful parallel to New Testament parables.

Borg, Marcus J. *Meeting Jesus Again for the First Time: The Historical Jesus and the Heart of Contemporary Faith.* San Francisco: HarperSanFrancisco, 1994; *Jesus: A New Vision: Spirit, Culture, and the Life of Discipleship*. San Francisco: Harper & Row, 1987. Using conclusions from modern historical-critical scholarship, Borg presents an engaging picture of the historical Jesus and the "Christ of faith" that he says arose in the church's reflections after the Resurrection.

Crossan, John Dominic. *The Historical Jesus: The Life of a Mediterranean Jewish Peasant.* San Francisco: HarperSanFrancisco, 1991. A good example of radical historical-skeptical reconstruction of the historical Jesus. Most valuable for its information about the first-century world.

Funk, Robert W., ed. *New Gospel Parallels.* Foundations and Facets Series. Philadelphia, Pa.: Fortress Press, 1985. All the extant Gospel material, canonical and noncanonical. A valuable resource.

Johnson, Luke Timothy. *The Real Jesus: The Misguided Quest for the Historical Jesus and the Truth of the Traditional Gospels.* San Francisco: HarperSanFrancisco, 1996. A mainstream Christian scholar argues against radical historical skepticism.

Kater, John L. Jr. *Jesus, My Mentor: A Spirituality for Living.* St. Louis, Mo.: Chalice Press, 2004. A clear, concise guide to the social dimensions of the Jesus' proclamation of the reign of God.

McKnight, Scot. *A New Vision for Israel: The Teachings of Jesus in National Context.* Grand Rapids, Mich.: Wm. B. Eerdmans

Publishing Co., 1999. A thorough scholarly investigation of the political dimensions of Jesus' message. See also McKnight's *The Jesus Creed: Loving God, Loving Others.* Brewster, Mass.: Paraclete Press, 2004. A fresh evangelical reading of Jesus' teachings organized around Jesus' simple "creed": Love God, neighbor, self.

Pagels, Elaine. *The Gnostic Gospels.* New York: Vintage/Random House, 1981. A concise presentation of the view that the growing orthodox party in the church suppressed a more vital, inclusive form of Christianity.

Robinson, James. M., ed. *The Nag Hammadi Library in English.* New York: Harper & Row, 1988. The scholar's guide to alternative material.

Spoto, Donald. *The Hidden Jesus: A New Life.* New York: St. Martin's Press, 1998. A haunting, beautifully written, faithfilled journey to the heart of Jesus message, in spite of its high skepticism about the historical authenticity of much Gospel material.

Taylor, Brian C. *Becoming Human: Core Teachings of Jesus.* Cambridge, Mass.: Cowley Publications, 2005. A down-to-earth approach that uses paraphrases to get at the everyday, human level of living out Jesus' teachings.

About the Author

R OBERT CORIN MORRIS, an Episcopal priest, is founder and executive director of Interweave, an ecumenical and interfaith community learning center. Interweave teaches skills for holistic living that deepen spirituality, promote wellness, and support the common good. Robert Morris graduated from Yale University, received his STB from The General Theological Seminary and the Certificate in Spiritual Direction from Shalem Institute for Spiritual Formation. His extensive study in Jungian psychology and Judaism, particularly the mystical tradition, has influenced his understanding of the Gospels. Morris has served as a parish priest in Michigan and New Jersey and as a spiritual formation consultant to many churches in various denominations around the country. He is a regular contributor to *Weavings: A Journal of the Christian Spiritual Life* and author of two previous books, *Wrestling with Grace: A Spirituality for the Rough Edges of Daily Life* (Upper Room, 2003) and *Suffering and the Courage of God: Exploring How Grace and Suffering Meet* (Paraclete, 2005).

Other Titles of Interest

Creating a Life with God:
The Call of Ancient Prayer Practices
by Daniel Wolpert

Wolpert describes twelve prayer practices and explores how each can contribute to your journey of spiritual formation. Practices include silence, *lectio divina*, the Jesus prayer, creativity, and journaling. Guidance for both individuals and groups.

ISBN 0-8358-9855

Creativity and Divine Surprise:
Finding the Place of Your Resurrection
by Karla M. Kincannon

Kincannon invites readers to understand themselves as spiritual pilgrims and artists. Discover how to be more available for encounters with yourself, the world, and God, sensing the Holy in all things.

ISBN 0-8358-9812-1

A Mile in My Shoes: Cultivating Compassion
by Trevor Hudson

Hudson explains how we can be on pilgrimage in our own communities and cultivate compassion for people in our midst who are in pain.

ISBN 0-8358-9815

Shaped by the Word:
The Power of Scripture in Spiritual Formation
by M. Robert Mulholland, Jr.

Mulholland demonstrates how our approach to scripture can have a transforming effect upon our lives.

ISBN 0-8358-0936-6

Tending the Seed:
Nurture Your God-Given Potential
by Ann Siddall and Gary Stuckey

An engaging six-session small group study based on the Parable of the Sower. The authors use the metaphor of tending seeds to lead readers into spiritual formation practices.

ISBN 0-8358-9829

The Way of Transforming Discipleship
by Trevor Hudson and Stephen D. Bryant

A small-group study that challenges Christians to live the whole gospel by connecting spirituality and discipleship. South African pastor Trevor Hudson is a leading voice of reconciliation in his home country.

Participant's Book ISBN 0-8358-9842
Leader's Guide ISBN 0-8358-9841

Available from your local bookstore

online at www.UpperRoom.org/bookstore

or call 1-800-972-0433

Also by Robert Morris

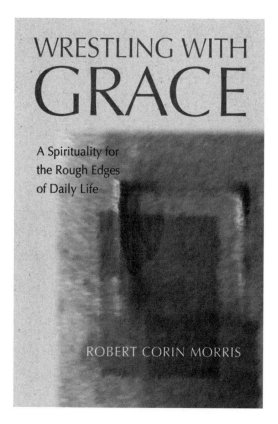

Wrestling with Grace: A Spirituality for the Rough Edges of Every-day Life offers insight into the daily practice of Christian spirituality. Robert Morris encourages us to learn how to bless the undesirables in our lives. When we do, we open our spirits to deeper joy and love.

ISBN 0-8358-0985-4